HOW ROBOTS INFLUENCE SERVICE NEED

JOHN LOK

ISBN 979-888591476-5

Contents

Preface

Introduction

What are our social customer and economic problems usually we will encounter in our lives. Can economists apply any economic theories to attempt to solve any economic or customer problems absolutely? Do economists apply any economic theories to solve any business problems in any economic environment or situations or they need find the suitable economic theories to solve the suitable environment of economic or customer problems?

Whether can apply behavioral economic method to raise productivity, service performance in organizations and predict consumer individual emotion in consumption market.

This book concerns to be given my opinions to explain how to apply demand and supply theory to analyze future artificial intelligent technological need on manufacturing and service industries aspect more as well as how to influence human job market change on service and manufacturing industries tasks aspects to be replaced by robotics in demand and supply view.

Prologue

Table of content

CHAPTER ONE

How applying economy theories solve economic problems

The economic problem – sometimes called the basic or central economic problem – asserts that an economy's finite resources are insufficient to satisfy all human wants and needs. Economics involves the study of how to allocate resources in conditions of scarcity However, viewing economics as the study of how society allocates resources can lead to conflation of normative economic planning and empirical study of how economic agents operate in these conditions.

In mainstream neoclassical economics, it is assumed that humans pursue their self-interest, and that the market mechanism best satisfies the various wants different individuals might have. These wants are often divided into individual wants (which depend on the individual's preferences and purchasing power parity) and collective wants (which are the wants of entire groups of people). Things such as food and clothing can be classified as either wants or needs, depending on what type and how often a good is requested.

However, economists have sometimes characterized "how" to produce as a "technological problem" of efficiency whereas the allocation of what is produced is an "economic problem". In a free market, the "how" of production and allocation of resources is distributed among economic agents. In a centrally planned economy, a principal decides how and what to produce on behalf of agents. Modern economies are often welfare capitalist with various regulations, which makes the economic system more equitable while retaining the distributed free market system. Due to human wants are unlimited, an infinite series of human wants remains continue with human life. Nobody can claim that all of his wants have been satisfied and he has no need to satisfy any further want. Everybody feels hunger at a time then other he needs water. Sometime one feels the desire of clothing then starts to feel the desire of having good conveyance. When all existing wants are satisfied then new wants starts to create in mind, so the series of wants remains continue till the last moment of life. So an economic problem arises because of existence of unlimited human wants.

● Problem of allocation of resources

The problem of allocation of resources arises due to the scarcity of resources, and refers to the question of which wants should be satisfied and which should be left unsatisfied. In other words, what to produce and how much to produce. More production of a good implies more resources required for the production of that good, and resources are scarce. These two facts together mean that, if a society decides to increase production of some good, it has to withdraw some resources from the production of other goods. In other words, more production of a desired commodity can be made possible only by reducing the quantity of resources used in the production of other goods.

The problem of allocation deals with the question of whether to produce capital goods or consumer goods. If the community decides to produce capital goods, resources must be withdrawn from the production of consumer goods. In the long run, however, [investment] in capital goods augments the production of consumer goods. Thus, both capital and consumer goods are important. The problem is determining the optimal production ratio between the two.

In fact, in our societies, resources are scarce and it is important to use them as efficiently as possible. Thus, it is essential to know if the production and distribution of national product made by an economy is maximally efficient. The production becomes efficient only if the productive resources are utilized in such a way that any reallocation does not produce more of one good without reducing the output of any other good. In other words, efficient distribution means that redistributing goods cannot make anyone better off without making someone else worse off. (See Pareto efficiency.) So, scientists will apply efficient distribution methods to help any countries to earn the absolute advantages when we buy and sell any kinds of products or food between ourselves countries, e.g. when US has good natural resource to grow any food, e.g. potato, wheat , vegetable, cotton , then

US can export to sell to China, because China has no any farms to grow agriculture food to supply itself Chinese to eat. So, China must need to buy any agriculture food from US. Otherwise, China has cheap labor to supply to US any manufacturers to help them to manufacture their electronic products. SO, it has many US factories are built in China to let Chinese workers help them to produce their products because their wages are cheaper to compare US workers. So, comparative economic advantage will be choice to apply between US and China both countries. (Absolute advantage trade theory)

The inefficiencies of production and distribution exist in all types of economies. The welfare of the people can be increased if these inefficiencies are ruled out. Some cost must be incurred to remove these inefficiencies. If the cost of removing these inefficiencies of production and distribution is more than the gain, then it is not worthwhile to remove them.

● The problem of full employment of resources

In view of how to use available resources are fully utilized is an important one. A community should achieve maximum satisfaction by using the scarce resources in the best possible manner—not wasting resources or using them inefficiently. There are two types of employment of resources:

(1) Labour-intensive

(2) Capital-intensive

In capitalist economies, however, available resources are not fully used. In times of depression, many people want to work but can't find employment. It supposes that the scarce resources are not fully utilized in a capitalistic economy.

● The problem of economic growth

If productive capacity grows, an economy can produce progressively more goods, which raises the standard of living. The increase in productive capacity of an economy is called economic growth. There are various factors affecting economic growth. The problems of economic growth have been discussed by numerous growth models, including the Harrod-Domar model, the neoclassical growth models of Solow and Swan, and the Cambridge growth models of Kaldor and Joan Robinson. This part of the economic problem is studied in the economies of development.

● Needs and wants problems

Needs are things or material items of peoples need for survival, such as food, clothing, housing, and water. Everyone has a different needs and wants. Until the Industrial Revolution, the vast majority of the world's population struggled for access to basic human needs.

Wants are effective desires for a particular product, or for something that can only be obtained by working for it. While the fundamental needs of survival are key in the function of the economy, wants are the driving force that stimulates demand for goods and services. To curb the economic problem, economists must classify the nature and different wants of consumers, as well as prioritize wants and organize production to satisfy as many wants as possible.

● Five bases problems of economy

In our societies , in general, our societies will have these similar problems The following points highlight the five basic problems of an economy. The problems are: 1. What to Produce and in What Quantities? 2. How to Produce these Goods? 3. For whom is the Goods Produced? 4. How Efficiently are the Resources being utilized? 5. Is the Economy Growing?.

Problem 1:What to Produce and in What Quantities?

The first central problem of an economy is to decide what goods and services are to be produced and in what quantities. This involves allocation of scarce resources in relation to the composition of total output in the economy. Since resources are scarce, the society has to decide about the goods to be produced: wheat, cloth, roads, television, power, buildings, and so on. Once the nature of goods to be produced is decided, then their quantities are to be decided. How many tones of wheat, how many televisions, how many million of power, how many buildings, etc. Since the resources of the economy are scarce, the problem of the nature of goods and their quantities has to be decided on the basis of priorities or preferences of the society.

If the society gives priority to the production of more consumer goods now, it will have less in the future. A higher priority on capital goods implies less consumer goods now and more in the future. But since resources are scarce, if some goods are produced in larger quantities, some other goods will have to be produced in smaller quantities. Suppose the economy produces capital goods and consumer goods. In deciding the total output of the economy, the society has to choose that combination of capital goods and consumer goods which is in keeping with its resources.

Problem 2: How to Produce these Goods?

The next basic problem of an economy is to decide about the techniques or methods to be used in order to produce the required goods. This problem is primarily dependent upon the availability of resources within the economy. If land is available in abundance, it may have extensive cultivation. If land is scarce, intensive methods of cultivation may be used. If labour is in abundance, it may use labour- intensive techniques; while in the case of labour shortage, capital-intensive techniques may be used.

The technique to be used also depends upon the type and quantity of goods to be produced. For producing capital goods and large outputs, complicated and expensive machines and techniques are required. On the other hand, simple consumer goods and small outputs require small and less expensive machines and comparatively simple techniques.

Further, it has to be decided what goods and services are to be produced in the public sector and what goods and services in the private sector. But in choosing between different methods of production, those methods should be adopted which bring about an efficient allocation of resources and increase the overall productivity in the economy.

Problem 3. For whom is the Goods Produced?

The third basic problem to be decided is the allocation of goods among the members of the society. The allocation of basic consumer goods or necessities and luxuries comforts and among the household takes place on the basis of among the distribution of national income. Whosoever possesses the means to buy the goods may have then. A rich person may have a large share of the luxuries goods, and a poor person may have more quantities of the basic consumer goods he needs.

Problem 4: How Efficiently are the Resources being Utilised?

This is one of the important basic problems of an economy because having made the three earlier decisions, the society has to see whether the resources it owns are being utilized fully or not. In case the resources of the economy are lying idle, it has to find out ways and means to utilize them fully.

Problem 5: Is the Economy Growing?

The last and the most important problem is to find out whether the economy is growing through time or is it stagnant. If the economy is stagnant at any point inside the production possibility curve, it has to be moved on to the production possibility curve PP whereby the economy now produces larger quantities of consumer goods and capital goods. Economic growth takes place through a higher rate of capital formation which consists of replacing existing capital goods with new and more productive ones by adopting more efficient production techniques or through innovations.

All of these economy problems will be our societies often causes to anyone feels need to solve problems in order to achieve our societies can have enough resources to satisfy our every day living.

● The Consumer Problem

Consumer theory is concerned with how a rational consumer would make consumption decisions. What makes this problem worthy of separate study, apart from the general problem of choice theory, is its particular structure that allows us to derive economically meaningful results. The structure arises because the consumer's choice sets are assumed to be defined by certain prices and the consumer's income or wealth. The consumer's problem is to choose that is most preferred or, equivalently, that has the greatest utility.

The assumption of perfect information is built deeply into the formulation of this choice problem, just as it is in the underlying choice theory. Some alternative models treat the consumer as rational but uncertain about the products, for example how a particular food will taste or a how well a cleaning product will perform. Some goods may be experience goods which the consumer can best learn about by trying ("experiencing") the good. In that case, the consumer might want to buy some now and decide later whether to buy more. That situation would need a different formulation. Similarly, if the agent thinks that high price goods are more likely to perform in a satisfactory way, that, too, would suggest quite a different formulation. Agents are price-takers. The agent takes prices p as known, fixed and exogenous. This assumption excludes things like searching for better prices or bargaining for a discount.

Hence , it seems that economic problems and consumer problems are similar, I feel that it is possible , economists can attempt to apply any economic theories to solve some consumer problems in some situations. They can find the accurate solutions when they can apply the suitable economic theories to solve the suitable consumer or economic problems in our societies. I shall indicate that how economists can apply the suitable economic theories to attempt to solve some consumer problems in our societies as below:

Demand And Supply Theory Solves Consumer Problems

What is economy rule predict consumer behaviour? Why and How does economist can apply economy rule to predict consumer behaviours? I shall explain the reasons as below:

Why does economic principle be the best to predict consumer behaviour. It may include these two reasons: The first focuses on the substantive domain of study, in this interpretation , economics is a social science devoted to understanding how the economy works. The second definition focuses on methods: economics is a way of doing social science, using particular tools. In this interpretation the discipline is associated with formal modelling and statistical analysis rather than particular hypotheses or theories about the economy. Therefore, economic methods can be applied to many other areas besides the economy, everything from decisions within the family to questions about political institutions.

● Demand and supply principle predict public transport tool passenger behaviour

Economists need to use the right economic ideas to predict consumer behaviour. So, Misuse the wrong economy ideas to predict consumer behaviours. It will do more wrong judgement to evaluate or predict why and how and when the country's consumer behaviours will change. It is every economist needs to consider issue. For example, the economy idea application of economic supply-demand principles to public transport. Different fares would give commuters with more-flexible hours the incentive to avoid peak travel times. They would allow passenger traffic to spread out over time, reducing the pressure on the public transport system when enabling even larger total passenger flow. IT aims to reduce traffic congestion, increased public-transport use, reduced car-bon emissions and cause air pollution and generated considerable revenue for the country's transport system. So, if the country can apply supply and demand economic principle to attempt to predict how many passengers number needs to catch transport tools to go to work or go to school or other activities. Then, it can predict how many bus, ferry, taxi, train, underground train, tram etc. different public transport tools to satisfy future public transport passengers' needs in society. So, this demand and supply principle is the comparative best rule to predict any kinds of public transport passengers' road needs, when they need to either go to school, go to office, go to leisure or shopping etc. different kinds of activities. So, applying the demand and supply principle to predict road and sea public transport passengers can help the country to reduce air pollution when they feel that they can find any public transport tools to catch any time conveniently , then it can encourage them to reduce car purchase desire. When many people choose to catch public transport tools, then it will reduce many cars number on the road. Then, air pollution will reduce as well as any public transport tools' income will also increase as well as traffic jam will also reduce. When the country can evaluate how many people choose to catch bus or taxi or ferry or train or underground train, or tram or train etc. different kinds of public transport tools, then the country can predict the more accurate public transport tools number to every kind of public transport tool to satisfy their journey needs. e.g. whether underground train or train or tram need to decrease or increase the frequent times or number to catch the volume of passenger in busy or non-busy time; or whether bus company has need to increase how much buses to catch the city location passengers when they are living in the city. Moreover, supply and demand principle can help any public transport tools to explain why their passengers number reduces in the year, it may due to fare charge is unreasonable, feeling uncomfortable to sit on the seat or air condition is poor in the transport tool environment, or there are no more seats because many there are much time is full passenger and no seat vacancy to provide to them to sit . So, supply and demand principle can help any kinds of public transport tools to find whether which is (are) the factor(S) can influence the current or last year passengers number reduce. Then, they can concentrate on improving their weaknesses to raise their service quality . So, supply and demand principle can also help they to evaluate whether what their weakness are in order to improve to increase passengers number. They can do questionnaires to enquiry their passengers' response to evaluate whether which areas of services that they feel unsatisfactory. So, the different kinds of service satisfactory feeling to the passengers number data will be the main source to help the kind of public transport tool to analyse and conclude the results more accurate, then they can make the more accurate judgement to improve the of service. For example, the questionnaires indicate that the many passengers feel the bus fare is reasonable, but many passengers feel they can not find any seats to sit easily. So, it implies that the bus firm ought buy more buses or enlarges bus size and increases more seats in the enlarged buses. Then, it does not reduce its fare but it needs to find solutions to let passengers can find seats to sit in every bus more easily. But, if the questionnaires indicate that there are many passengers feel its fare is higher or unreasonable to compare other kinds of public transportation tools. Hence, it can avoid to spend more expenditure to increase bus number to the city, if the city has many passengers , they still choose bus to catch, but they feel its fare is too higher to compare other kinds of public transport tool. Then, it only needs to reduce its fare , it ought help it to increase passengers number. Hence, demand and supply principle is the most suitable economic method to evaluate any kinds of public transport system passenger needs in any country nowadays.

● Supply and demand and price elasticities principle predict oil energy user behaviour

The another case is that demand and supply principle can predict oil buyer behaviour to find whether what factors can cause the oil buyer individual need reduces. For example , a rise in production costs increases market prices and reduces quantities demanded and supplied. Or when, energy cost rise, utility bills increases and households fid extra ways of saving heating and electricity. But, others are nor. For example, whether a tax is imposed on the producers or consumer of a commodity, say oil has nothing to do with who ends up paying for it. The tax might be administered on oil companies, but it might be consumers who really pay for it through higher prices at the pump. Or the extra cost might be imposed on consumers in the form of a sale tax, but the oil companies might be forces to absorb it through lower prices. It all depends on the " price elasticities" of demand and supply. With the addition of extra assumption, this model also generates rather strong implications about how well markets work. In particular, a competitive market economy is efficient in the sense that it is impossible to improve one person's well-being without reducing somebody.

● Demand and supply principle can misuse to predict consumer behaviour when the two firms participate advertisement to promote their products in the same time

Why can demand and supply principle misuse to predict consumer behaviour when the two firms participate advertisement to promote their products in the same time ? I shall explain as below: Assume that two competing firms must decide whether to have a big advertising budget. Advertising would allow one firm to steal some of the other's customers.

But when they both advertise, the effects on customer demand cancel out. The firms end up having spent money needlessly.

We might expect that neither firm would choose to spend much on advertising, but the model shows that this logic is off base. When the firms make their choices independently and they care only about their own profits, each one has an incentive to advertise, regardless of what the other firm does. When the other firm does not advertise, you can steal customers from it if you do advertise, when the other firm does advertise, you have to advertise to prevent loss of customers. So, these two firms end up in a bad equilibrium in which both have to waste resources. This market can not apply demand and supply principle to predict consumer behaviours because they depends advertisement to promote their products. If these two firms advertise their products in the same time. Then , it is not possible that if one firm increases it price and it will cause its customer number loss, due to its advertise can help it to attract customers to consider its product from television or radio or newspapers or magazine promotion channels. So, I suppose that these two firms decide to increase their price, when they advertise their products to let customers to know in the same time. They will not lose their customers or reduce their customers easily. Because their customers can be persuaded to choose to buy their products to compare other similar products in preference. So, their increasing price will not influence their customers number lose easily. It explains that demand and supply principle is not right to this case, so demand and supply principle can misuse to help them to predict consumer behaviours when they advertise their products in the same time. Also, demand and supply principle is not suitable to them to predict consumer behaviours when they advertise their products in the same time. They will do wrong prediction to their consumers purchase desire when they advertise their products in the same time.

ON conclusion, using these demand and supply and price elasticity techniques, economists derive specific prediction for how consumers choose which products to buy, how households save, how firms invest, how workers search for jobs, as well as for how these actions depend on the particulars. They can help them to predict job and consumption behaviours more accurate, it depends on whether the situation is right, such as both competition firms participate to advertise their products in the same time case, it is not right to apply above economic principle to predict consumer behaviours. They will get wrong prediction when they apply this principle to predict consumer behaviours.

However, demand and supply principle can predict below any one of these cases. I shall indicate as below:

The problem of need-based scholarships: Most systems for providing college scholarships are based on some definition of financial needs, with scholarships generally being given only to those students who must need financial help in order to attend school.

Is need, rather than academic ability, the best basic on which to choose those students who are to be encouraged to attend college? Which way of choosing who gets aids is the more just? Which is the more efficient ? Is the overall educational level of society increased more by giving financial aid to bright students or to needy students? Presumably the aid offers more leverage to needy students, since they all need the money in order to attend college, whereas, many of the bright students would attend college in any case. But is a smaller number of bright students the more important addition?

So, the school can apply demand and supply principle to predict whether how many parents feel need financial assistance and evaluate how much financial amount is the right to borrow. It aims to calculate how many parents feel real financial need and how much to lend to them in order to let these students to get the most fair financial assistance.

Assuming the school wish to use need as a basis, how does the school determines " financial need"?

Is need a function or parents' income? What, then , does the school about children of wealthy parents who are living independently of them and get no aid from parents? Should they be punished for their parents' wealth? But if they are given aid, won't all students, in order to get aid, claim to be independent of their parents?

Is need solely a matter of family income, or should not the school takes a family's financial obligations into account? Does not it make more sense to give aid to someone whose parents must put night more children through school than to someone from a family of five or one only with the same income? But in a possible parallel situations, should a family that carries mortgages on one or two large homes get preference simply because they do not have much money left to spend on college? Does doing this reward ? Is there a difference between the case of night children and the case of the large mortgage? How should parents who are not married , but are living together and supporting their children jointly be counted? Most parents are supporter to their children , although they are married in possible.

So, the school needs to gather all these data to evaluate how many parents are not married or married or living with their children together, how much salary they earn as well as every family has how much children as well as whether they have mortgage for their houses. So, these number will be the financial education assistance demanders, but it does not represent their real financial needs. It is possible that someone does not feel any financial need, although their children apply financial assistance to your school. Then , your school needs to evaluate whether how much financial assistance can lend to every real financial need student family. It can not exceed your final financial expenditure budget (supply) , when your financial expenditure is not enough. SO, demand and supply principle can be applied to research this school real family financial demand to lend to the real financial need families and evaluate whether the reasonable financial amount to lend to every child family to study in your school.

● Supply and demand principle applies to immigration to decide wage case

A fascinating and important example of supply and demand, full of complexities, is the role of immigration in determining wages. If you ask people , they are likely to tell you that immigration into California or Florida US, surely lowers the wages of people in those regions. It is just supply and demand analysis of immigration. According to this analysis, of these to these two regions in US. Immigration in to a region shifts the supply curve for labor to the right and pushes down wages. Why has it relationship between immigration to US these two regions immigrant number and wage?

Careful economic studies cast doubt on this simple proposition, however, a recent survey of the evidence concludes:

The effect of immigration on the labor market outcomes of natives is small in US. There is no evidence of economically significant reductions in native employment. Most analysis, finds that a 10 percent increase in the fraction of immigrants in the population reduced native wages by a most 1%.

How can we explain the small impact of immigration on wages? The main mistake is to forget how mobile the American population is and that the impact of immigration on wages, we must examine the effect of new immigrants when the strength of the local economy and the number of native-born residents in a city are unchanged, that is , when these other things are held constant. Unless you exclude the effects other changing variables, you can not accurately predict the impact of immigration. The same principle holds in doing a supply0and demand analysis of any market. As much as possible, when you are examining the impact of a supply or demand shift, you must try to keep all other things constant.

● Rationing by prices

By determining the equilibrium prices and quantities of all inputs and outputs, the market allocated or rations out the scare goods of the society among the possible uses. Who does the rationing? A planning board? Congress or the president? BO, the marketplace, through the interaction of supply and demand, doe the rationing. This is rationing by the purse.

What foods are produces? This is answered by the signals of the market price. High oil prices stimulates oil production, whereas low food prices drive resources out of agriculture. Those who have the most dollars votes have the greatest influences on what goods are produced. All of these considers how demand and supply to the market.

For whom are goods produces? The power of the pursue indicates the distribution of income and consumption. Those with higher incomes end up with larger houses, more clothing, and linger vacations. When the most urgently felt needs get fulfilled through the demand curve.

Even, the how question is decided by supply and demand. When corn prices are low, it is not profitable for farmers to use expensive tractors and irrigation systems, and only the best land is cultivated. When oil prices are high, oil companies drill in deep offshore waters and employ novel seismic techniques to find oil.

IN sum , any thing needs through demands, interact with costs of goods, as reflected in supplies in our economic world. Hence, demand and supply theory ought be the most accurate method to help any businesses or governments to predict their shareholders behaviours when they will change as well as how and how their behaviours change.

Consumer choice theory solves consumer problems

What is 'consumer choice theory'?

'Consumer choice theory' is a hypothesis about why people buy things. Put simply, it says that you choose to buy the things that give you the greatest satisfaction, while keeping within your budget. At the heart of this theory are three assumptions about human nature.[1]

The first assumption is that when you shop, you choose to buy things based on calculated decisions about what will make you happiest. In economics language, this is known as utility maximisation (Economists really like to put quite simple concepts into long complicated terms.)

Secondly, the theory assumes that no matter how much you shop, you will never be completely satisfied. In other words, you will always be happier consuming a little bit more. This is known as the principle of non-satiation. Thirdly, even though you always get more happiness from more consumption, the amount of pleasure you get from each good decreases with the more you consume. So if you eat two ice creams rather than one, you get more overall pleasure, but the second ice-cream won't be as satisfying as the first. This is known as decreasing marginal utility.

Consumer choice theory has influenced everything from government policy to corporate advertising to academia. But the theory has been criticized for not being the most accurate description of how people actually make choices. A whole new branch of economics, called 'behavioral economics', has emerged essentially to use findings from psychology to disprove the assumptions behind consumer choice theory. This has also led others to argue that consumer choice theory is less about describing how we do actually behave, and is more about describing how people should behave.[3] In other words, by portraying people as self-interested shopaholics, economists are saying that is it okay and natural for us to be avid consumers.

● Consumer choice theory can be applied to solve consumer problems during the country can have economic growth , the reasons may include as below:

The scenario leading to inflation starts with poor growth. Forget about everything that comes next and focus on that most important factor. Because it happens that the scenario leading to a budget crisis also starts with poor growth, and the scenario leading to a long-term unemployment crisis starts with poor growth, and a scenario leading to a better-the-neighbor trade crisis starts with poor growth, and so on. So a very important question is: what can be done to improve the prospects for economic growth? In particular, what is the right countercyclical approach to take to best situate the economy for future growth? I shall indicate during US, America's economy growth occurs, then economists can attempt to apply customer choice theory to solve US itself country's consumer problems more easier.

In no small part, the question comes down to interpretations of charts like the one at right. On the one hand, long and deep downturns seem to have almost no effect on the long-term rate of growth. On the other hand, in the long run we're all dead, and those who live during an extended period of economic weakness suffer for it. Meanwhile, it's also difficult to see where high debt levels influence the long-run rate of growth, at least where this chart is concerned.

During to the medium-term growth stage, is the bigger threat to American growth rates a market revolt against American debt levels? Or is it structural unemployment stemming from the slow, jobless recovery? Or is the cyclical shortfall in public investment? Or something else entirely? Of course, there's no real reason one has to choose a problem to address at the expense of others. More aggressive monetary expansion could make the finding of a solution to all these problems easier, but the Fed is unwilling to oblige me on this score. It may well be concerned that lack of fiscal discipline will lead to increasing inflation expectations, making its job harder (but then fiscal problems are trace able to growth). If that is the worry, however, one has to ask why the Congress has been unable to strike a deal for $20 billion in stimulus this year for $80 billion in fiscal tightening in a year or two (fill in whatever amounts you wish). But the outlook for the American economy vis-a-vis any number of potential crises will hinge on growth, and growth will hinge on the ability of private business to exploit promising opportunities as they arise. And the question is: what's likely to hurt that ability most? High interest rates? Lack of consumer demand? A shortage of adequately prepared workers? Right now firms appear to be most worried about demand shortfalls. So how much can you boost demand without making the primary fear high interest rates? A lot, if the expansion is on the monetary side.

● How to supply consumer choice theory to predict Consumer Behavior Marketing at Apple Computer

During US economy growth, Apply computer applies consumer choice theory to solve its computer buyers' choice problems among different kinds of brand computer competitors. Have you ever wondered why Apple is so successful? They were not the first company to invent the personal computer, portable music device, the tablet, the smartphone, software to download music, or the set-top box to name a few. Apple has amassed a brand loyal following like no other brand backed by significant sales, market share, and profitability. So, how does Apple do it? What's the secret behind their success?

Marketing using consumer behavior insight is how Apple succeeds. Even though Steve Jobs and Apple, did not use consumer research in the initial development of most products, consumer behavior plays a huge role in their marketing and ultimately the success of the company. Once a consumer purchases a product or downloads iTunes Apple has access to data the company leverages. Apple uses this information to gain significant insight into the consumer and what drives purchase behavior.

Consumer behavior marketing is an essential ingredient in the current business climate. The companies that apply this type of marketing well have a distinct competitive advantage that distances them from their rivals. Consumer behavior research is the primary driver at the core of any good strategy. Research provides actionable insight and ensures business success. If you answer no to the following questions, this post is for you?

•Are you applying consumer behavior marketing currently?

•Have you conducted consumer behavior research within the last two years?

•Do you have consumer behavior marketing in your marketing plan with well-defined marketing strategies and tactics?

•Are you achieving the maximum results for your organization?

Every business has a target audience and consumer behavior marketing provides the fundamental methods for understanding your target. Consumer behavior research provides the underlying element that drives quality strategies and ensures business results.

"Marketing is understanding your buyers really, really well. Then creating valuable products, services, and information especially for them to help solve their problems."

The organizations that have an intimate understanding of their target audience possess a competitive advantage over those that do not. Establishing a one-to-one relationship and thorough knowledge of your target audience is a core responsibility for business in the 21st century and beyond. Regardless if you are B2B, B2C, B2G or a hybrid organization you have a target audience. The information in this post can be applied to any business type. This post focuses on Apple (B2C) employing consumer behavior marketing as a critical ingredient for their success.

Hence, Apply computer shops have several computer teachers to teach any visitors how to use its laptops, hen they enquire its any computer salespeople. Due to its salespeople had been trained to learn how to use the different kinds of laptops. So, anyone enquires them, they can answer their enquires concern any computer questions immediately. Then, they will feel Apple laptops are the first choice to compare other kinds of laptops brands. It is one salespeople answering strategies to persuade any Apple computer visitors to feel its any laptops are the first or preference choice to compare its competitors in this computer market, so customer choice economic theory is the most suitable strategy to solve Apple computer's customer individual purchase decision problem.

Microeconomics Models and Theories solve customer problems

Microeconomics is concerned with the economic decisions and actions of individuals and firms. Within the broad church of microeconomics, there are different theories that certain assumptions and expectations of economic behaviour. The most important theory is neo-classical theory, which places emphasis on free-markets and the assumption individuals are rational and seek to maximise utility. However, there are many critiques of the neo-classical model, arguing economics is more complex with issues of market failure and irrational behaviour.

Pre-classical microeconomic theory

Before, Adam Smith, economics was more disparate with no commanding overall theory. Philosophers like Aristotle and Plato made references to issues in economics such as division of labour. The dominant ideas, pre-classical economics, were based on theories of mercantilism – the idea a nation should try to accumulate gold.

Classical microeconomic theory

Classical microeconomic theory was developed by Adam Smith (Wealth of Nations, 1776) and later economists, such as David Ricardo The essential aspect of classical microeconomic theory include:

Adam Smith mentioned the 'invisible hand of the market.' He noted how when people act out of self-interest, markets tend to provide goods and services which are demanded by the population. It needed no central price setting, but market forces responded to changes in demand and supply, e.g. a shortage pushes up the price and causes demand to fall.

Smith also investigated topics such as the division of labour, specialisation and economies of scale. The early classical economists emphasised the importance of costs to firms and consumers.

Utility maximisation

An important development of classical economics towards the end of the nineteenth century is the concept of utility maximisation. The concept of utility was developed by philosophers/economists – Jeremy Bentham and John Stuart Mill. In microeconomic theory, it was believed a consumer will buy goods depending on the marginal utility (satisfaction) they get from the good. This theory assumes consumers are rational and seeking to maximise the satisfaction they get.

Neo-classical theory

Neo-classical theory is a modern re-interpretation of classical economics of the nineteenth century. Neo-classical theory places importance on markets, but developed new ideas, especially regarding utility and rational choice theory. Elements of neo-classical theory.

1. Market distribution of goods and services.

2.R ational choice theory. This is the idea individuals hold rational preferences and make rational choices; seeking to maximise their outcomes – be it profit, wages, consumption or investment.

3. People act independently and make use of available information.

4. Marginalism. In neo-classical economics, more emphasis was placed on concepts of marginal utility and marginal cost. We make choices depending on satisfaction we get from one extra unit of a good.

Economists such as Carl Menger, William Stanley Jevons and Marie-Esprit-Léon Walras. and Alfred Marshall developed ideas such as diminishing marginal utility. Many of these neo-classical economic theories were brought together in Alfred Marshall's very influential textbook, Principles of Economics. (1890)

•Note there is some blurring between classical economics and neo-classical economics.

•Neo-classical economics has also come to mean 'orthodox economic theory. To a large extent, it has incorporated new developments in microeconomics, such as theories of market failure, market structure and econometrics.

Theories of Market failure

Neo-classical economics has become associated with a belief in the efficiency of markets. However, microeconomic theory has also incorporated the criticisms and limitations of free-markets.

•Monopoly. Adam Smith was well aware of the problem of monopolies and how firms could use their market power to set excessive prices.

•Imperfect competition. In the 1930s, Joan Robinson developed a model of imperfect competition, an awareness many markets were somewhere between monopoly and perfect competition often assumed in neo-classical economics.

•Externalities. Developed by Arthur C.Pigou in The Economics of Welfare (1920) this is the awareness production and consumption decisions can have harmful (or positive) effects on third parties. Therefore, a free market can lead to overconsumption of demerit goods and negative externalities.

•Game theory. An awareness, decisions are not linear or simple, but the interdependence of agents influences what we decide to do.

Behavioural economics

The most important trend in recent decades in economics is the greater emphasis placed on aspects of behavioural economics, which uses many insights from related fields such as psychology.

•Disputes rational choice theory. The essential element of behavioural economics is that it argues individual agents are often not rational and often do not seek to maximise utility.

•Behavioural economics examines how agents can be influenced by biases, and make decisions not predicted by neo-classical economic theory. Behavioural economics can explain the irrational exuberance of booms and busts.

Econometrics

In the post-war period, economics became increasingly mathematical with economists attempting to use mathematics to explain models and theories. Econometrics looks at economic data and seeks to extract simple relationships. The basic tool is the linear regression models and can be used to try and predict consumer spending and demand for labour.

Heterodox models of microeconomics

Heterodox models differ substantially from microeconomic foundations of neo-classical economics. Schools of thought include

Marxist economic theory

Karl Marx developed an alternative perspective on economics. He focused on the surplus value created under the capitalist economic system. To Marx, the invisible hand of the market would be better described as the invisible hand of capitalist exploitation of workers. Marx claimed workers did receive their full labour value but were compensated for their necessary labour only – enabling capitalists to profit from the surplus.

Institutional economics. The role of society and institutions in shaping economic behaviour. For example, Thomas Veblen looked at theories of 'conspicuous consumption' and noted how the desire for social status could drive much economic theory. Institutional economics could be seen as a forerunner for later behavioural economics.

Environmental economics Argues traditional economics wrongly places value on increasing output. The most important thing is creating a sustainable environment which maximises living standards. So, manufacturers need to consider how to manufacture their products , but pollution can not be raised as the same time, because human will face to raise cost of living and living experiences to be poor , even food shortage, water pollution , air pollution , death rate raises when technological productivities brings pollution to our natural environment. Hence, environmental economoic theory is the most suitable to solve manufacturers' pollution problem.

Buddhist economics/non-profit goals. Like environmental economics, this questions the assumption higher incomes and higher output are desirable. The theory of hedonistic relativism suggests higher incomes do nothing to increase happiness levels, and traditional economics can encourage society to pursue materialistic goals which actually create more problems of stress, conflict and environmental degradation.

Some of the basic models you might find in A-Level economics :

•Price Discrimination

•Perfect competition

•Price Mechanism

•Monopoly

•Oligopoly and kinked demand curve

•Game Theory Pricing strategies

•Market failure

•Behavioural economics

ON conclusion, any macro economy theories can be applied to find the most reasonable methods to solve any customer problems in societies by economists as above. So, I believe that any economic and customer and social problems can be solved by economic theories in our society.

Demand and supply theory solves social problems

Over the past 20 years, many researchers believe to apply behavioral economic macroeconomic models which can predict market behavioral change. The reasons are based on assumptions of optimizing behavior in many cases have difficulty accounting for key real-world observations. Hence, researchers have used behavioral economics assumptions with the aim of making their model predicting better fit the data. The reason for behavioral economics results into macroeconomics will be more accurate to predict market behavioral change in macro-economy view point, such as economic fluctuation prediction, the consumption, formation of expectations and determination of wages and employment how to aggregation supply and the possibility of consumer individual demand product or service number prediction more accurately.

● How to apply behavioral economy (demand and supply) theory to predict marketing behavioral changes more accurate?

Anyway, economists aim to develop models of human behavior and interactions in market in order to build useful models. Economists make simplifying assumptions to analyze why the market will be changed by consumer individual consumption behavior changing.

Why do I assume consumers are as economic man ? In behavioral economy view point, how the perception of the economic man's behavior (including consumer choices) of economic models with the development of economics as a science. Economists explain the concept of economics as a science. It is the concept of consumer as an economic man, the essence and complexity of consumer behavior.

The consumer and consumer purchasing behavior are an important area of interest of many scientific disciplines. The process of economic decision making as well as consumption choices are connected with wider human activities. The terms of both consumer individual attitudes and group social behavior will influence group social behavior will influence consumer individual final consumption decision in every consumption choice process. Thus, behavioral economy method can predict consumer behavioral changing, it can apply these sciences to research, includes sociology, psychology, anthropology, operational research, decision theory etc. different literature research aspects. I assume that businessmen can apply behavioral economy method to predict market changing behaviors successfully if they own behavioral economy knowledge.

In this part, I shall concentrate on explain how the perception of the economic man's behavior (including consumer choice) is applied to predict market behaviors. After explaining the concept of consumer as an economic man, the nature and complexity of consumer behavior are discussed to below different industries' marketing behavioral changing every case studies in US or UK countries.

Why is consumer as an economic man? IN behavioral economy view point, the concept of answer is one of the fundamental concepts in economics because the consumer is the case market participant along with the producer. In general, lecturers define the consumer in various ways, but in behavioral economy view point, consumers mean economy man. Because who will compare cost and benefit to any product or service to decide to choose to buy the product or consume the service. Consumers are as "economic man", who will make own subjective preferences (tastes), habits and traditions and existing objective constraints (i.e. disposal income) market prices of products and services in order to satisfy whose needs to a maximum degree and in the most rational way.

Thus, economic man means consumers need to make psychological mind to decide whether who either prefer to buy this product or another product or prefer to consume this service or another service more suitable. Thus, any markets or industries need have themselves benefits and consumers must need to evaluate whether the product or service has more benefits to compare other products or services in the consumption market to satisfy whose needs. It means that if the product or service has more benefits to compare other similar products or services. Then the product or service will persuade many consumers to choose to but the product or consume the service.

Consequently, in first part, I shall indicate how to apply behavioral economy theory : economic man psychological method, benefits and costs benefits method, how to predict these US and UK enterprises marketing behavioral changing more accurate.

In the second part, I shall apply micro employee behavioral economy concept to explain how to solve these US and UK inter-organizational management challenge.

I believe that behavioral economy method can be applied to research organizational employee behaviors change, e.g. how any why the employee chooses to do this action in whose organization. Moreover, behavioral economy method can be applied to consumption market to predict how any why the consumer choose to buy the product or consume the service. So, any consumers and employees personal psychology and external environment economic factor will influence how to choose to do decision in any organizations or consumption environment.

Bibliography

Bandiera, O., I. Barankay, and I. Rasul (2005). Social preferences and the response to incentives: Evidence from personal data. The quarterly journal of economics 120 (3), 917-969.

Exadaktylos, F., A.M. Espin and P. Branas-Garza (2013). Experimental subjects are not different. Scientific reports 3, 1213.

Lazear, E.P. (1979). Why is there mandatory retirement? Journal of political economy 87(6), 1261-1284.

● Behavioral economic method (demand and supply theory) predicts stable basic income consumer individual spending behavior

Can apply behavioral economic method to predict that the consequences of a stable basic income consumer's consumption behavior? It may be significantly different than the ones are predicted by the standard economic model if more realistic assumptions of human consumption behavioral prediction success.

Behavioral economic method assumes that consumer will compare whether whose benefits are more than costs after they buy the product or consume the service. I assume the consumer is only the who have stable basic income source consumer target. This stable basic income target consumers who will evaluate or feel they will earn more benefits than costs to every product in their consumption process, after they will make final decision to choose to buy the product to use or consume the service. Otherwise, if they feel they won't earn more benefits after they buy the product or consume the service in the consumption process. Then, they won't choose to buy the product to use or consume the service. In behavioral economic view point, it indicates their consumption behaviors are depend on comparing the product or the service whether it can satisfy their desire benefits and their desire benefits to the product or service must be more than their consumption cost.

There are four points to apply behavioral economic method to predict each stable basic income individual income spending. They include: motivation, conspicuous consumption, social preferences and crowding theory.

Each stable basic income consumer individual spending amount will be different and it is represent that every high stable basic income consumer must decide to consume any high cost services or buy high cost products to use. Although some economic teachers assume general high income people will accept to spend more expenditures for enjoyment or buy high cost of products to satisfy basic high level necessary expenditures. But, applying behavioral economic analysis, it is not absolute true, some low income people also accept to spend more to buy high cost of products or increasing spending expenditures for enjoyment for their basic necessary expenditures.

The field of behavioral economic can be fined as a combination of economics and psychology that tries to capture human behavior in a more realistic. Understanding each consumer individual consumption behavior, we need to know how who does each decision to influence each consumption choice. Consequently, analysis reaches the conclusion. Every high or low level stable basic income consumer individual behavioral consumption that the microeconomic consequences of a stable basic income of individual consumer target consumption group could be efficiency enhancing, but at the same time incentives about positional concerns could lead to wasteful and inefficient spending to the stable low basic income consumer target group.

● How to apply demand and supply theory to contribute to the stable basic income target consumer group's consumption prediction?

What is basic income mean? A basic income is an income paid by a political community to all its members on an individual basis, without means test or work requirement. How to apply behavioral economic method to contribute to the basic income consumption prediction?

I assume high income tax is charged to one high income tax payee , it will influence the high income tax payee individual consumption desires to be fallen, also extrinsic incentives will effort and intrinsic motivation and how the labor market change these variables under and big changes predicting, how income security changes social consumption preferences, e.g. how a big change affects the overall level of status -seeking behavior and this effect with income inequality to influence consumer individual consumption attitude or habit.

How can behavioral economic methods predict consumer's consumption decision, in special the stable basic income consumer target group? In any consumption decisions are involving risk and uncertainty, the standard economic model usually assumes that decisions are based on final condition, regardless of the changes are caused by the results of a consumer's decision.

An alterative mode of how consumers make decision and judgement under risk and uncertainty. This situation is often occurred in consumption market.

In behavioral economic view point, it explains how consumer's consumption, however, which excludes the stable basic income earn factor can influence the stable basic income earn target consumer group decides to make final consumption decision to compare to the non-stable basic income earn target consumer group. The reasons include as below:

(1) Consumers evaluate decisions over gains and losses with respect to some natural reference point, when they feel need to consume, which is assumed to be judgement about a sequence of outcomes are based on changes in wealth, rather than whether how much absolute basic income earn to influence whose consumption desires.

(2) Thus, behavioral economic theory assumes the consumer is the low level of income group in society, but when who feels that he is still gains more than losses when who decides to buy the expensive product or consumes the expensive service. Then, the low level of income consumer who will accept to buy the expensive product or consume the service easily. Due to whose gains feeling is more than losses feeling, when who buys the product or consumes the service.

(3) Behavioral economic theory also assumes the taxpayer will pay high income tax in this year. The, even the high income taxpayer can earn high basic income, but due to whom needs to pay high income tax in this year. Then, he/she will reduce much spending, even he/she reduces spending on cheap products or cheap service consumption for enjoyment. This is the taxpayer's economic decision to influence whose consumption behavior, due to the high income tax expenditure factor influences whose consumption behavior to change to be reduced spending expenditures in this year.

How to apply behavioral economic method to predict labor market changing behavior?

Instead of applying behavioral economic method to predict every consumer individual consumption effort. Behavioral economic method can be also be applied to predict every country's labor market changing behavior. Particularly, how salary clerical workers or low wage labor workers should move from one type of job to another based on these factors. They include as below:

Their intrinsic motivation and how their levels of effort would change after this movement, investigates the effects of income security on social preferences in labor market changing behavior, and how cooperation in social contribution is affected when income security is guaranteed, how to predict the role of positional externalities on conspicuous consumption and how would change the incentive to influence consumption. So, it seems that general labor market job changing behaviors will not influenced by external economic environment better or worse changing factor, or salary changing factor etc. different environmental condition changing factors influence to employees' job changing. Generally, employee's job changing behavior is more influenced to persuade who changes job by himself/herself intrinsic motivation negative emotion influence mainly.

How to apply motivation crowding theory to predict labor productivity? One of the main challenges of economic theory is to find what are the optimal incentives that increase productivity of labors. The standing point is usually extrinsic incentive be it is form of monetary compensations for high effort or fine for low effort.

It is a kind method of reward or punishment to increase or decrease number of productivity to every labor. But it can only raise short term number of productivity in possible and it can not guarantee high quality of productivity. So if one employer wants a labor to do more of an activity or with a higher quality, consider paying the labor for working hard on punishing whom if for providing a low level effort.

This idea is that people do not like to work, and therefore they used some sort of compensation for doing a specific activity, and that the more they are paid the harder, they will work. So, payment better compensation is only beneficial to encourage labors to do one specific task or activity in short term. This method can not be suitable to rise long term beneficial productivity and high level quality of production or excellent performance in long term and it can only keep in short term raising productivity and high level quality of production or excellent performance benefits.

Consider paying the labor for working hard on punishing whom if for providing a low level effort. This idea is that people do not like to work, and therefore they used some sort of compensation for doing a specific activity, and that the more they are paid the harder they will work. So, payment better compensation is only beneficial to encourage labors to do one specific task or activity in short term. This method can not be suitable to raise long them beneficial productivity and high quality of products.

However, economists would argue that, is a labor has high intrinsic motivative to perform a task, who will provide a high level of effort without compensation by himself/herself but an even higher level of effort of whom is compensated. If a labor does not have any intrinsic motivation to perform a task or an activity, who will provide no effort or a low effort of whom. There is no compensation, but who will increase this level of effort of an extrinsic incentive is implemented.

Hence, in behavioral economic view point, the labor individual high level effort is a main psychological factor to influence whose productivity to be raised or the qualities of products to be raised, when the products are manufactured by the high level effort labor. It means that high compensation is not the good method to encourage labor productivity or raise quality. Otherwise, how to influence the one low level of effort of labor to change to be one high level of effort labor. It is the best psychological method to influence the labor to raise productivity and quality and service performance to any products or services in manufacturing process or service process for any organizations in long term beneficial possible.

● How can apply demand and supply theory raises basic stable income consumer consumption desire

Economists aim to develop models of human behavior and interactions in consumption markets. But consumers behave in complex ways, such as how to predict consumers to make rational decisions in consumption processes. Moreover, self-consumption control and motivation can vary significantly across different individual consumer.

In order to build useful consumption prediction models, economists make simplifying assumptions, aims to predict how to raise stable basic income consumer target group consumption more success. However, behavioral economy method is one kind of accurate consumption prediction method. It can be applied to predict economic decision-making to every consumer consumption choice more accurate raising whose consumption desire?

I shall indicate how to apply different behavioral economy methods (demand and supply theory) to raise stable basic stable income target consumer group consumption desire in these different consumption situation (consumption environment) aspects as below:

1. Stable basic stable income consumer group consumption great or small amount desire

The consumption of products and services is a fundamental part of consumer's welfare. Basically, every one who has stable basic stable income, who will like to consume any products and services. Even, consumption great or small amount desire won't be depended on whether the person whose income is more or less. It means low income level of people will still like to consume great amount to buy expensive products or consume expensive services, because consumption is human's part of life and basic needs.

This stable basic income people will like to consume, because they have stable income source when they do not worry about unemployment occurrence to cause them have no enough money to support their life. Otherwise, non-stable basic stable income people won't like to consume because they feel they have no stable basic income source to support their life and they will worry about unemployment occurrence any time. Hence, stable basic income people will have more consumption desire to compare non-stable basic stable income people in any countries usually. Behavioral economic method indicates they feel their economic benefits will be loss if they planned to buy any products or consume any services easily. So, they prefer to save money in bank more than consumption.

1. Demand systems and micro-economic factor influence basic income people consumption attitude

Why stable basic income people will like to consume? Because who have more demand, a demand system shows the level of consumer demand for different products and services: e.g. one basic stable income person may refer to the demand for clothes, another the demand for food etc.

How the demand for that particular product varies with the prices and demographic factor will influence who to accept consumption. Such as stable basic income people who will not consider to decide to buy the cloth to wear or the food to eat if who feel the cloth or food price is even more expensive to compare other kind of cloth or food.

Otherwise, non-stable basic income people who will consider to decide to buy the cloth to wear or the food to eat if they feel that they still have enough cloths to wear or enough food to eat at homes , even these food or cloth price are less expensive to compare others. Because they feel they lack stable income effort to support them to consume. Hence, basic stable income factor can influence the consumer's consumption decision.

2. Life-cycle advertisement method can influence consumer individual consumption behaviors to be increased

Consumer behavior makes strong assumptions about the informational and computational bases of consumer behavior. Generally, consumer behavior is reasonably characterized as the maximization of expected lifetime utility subject to budget constraint and conditional on the available information.

Generally, consumers prefer to buy any discounted products or it is reasonable that consumers accept to buy many attractions to persuade them to buy any kinds of bargain discount products. Hence, low bargain discount product is one good behavioral economic principle to encourage or persuade or attract any consumers to increase consumption.

What is behavioral life-cycle model? This model explains consumer behavior can be persuaded to buy any discounted products by advertisement, e.g. television, radio, newspapers, magazine etc. promotion channels. Because frequent advertisement promotion method can let any consumers often remember the product's brand, discounted price, style, color and image from advertisement content.

So, advertisement can be one part of consumer behavioral life-cycle. For example, when the television audiences often watch TV. Hence, when the brand of product advertisement often makes fun image and discounted message to let TV audiences to remember this brand of product, when they are watching TV. Then, it has possible to persuade any potential consumers to choose to buy this brand of any products or consume this brand of any services, due to its advertisement of discounted sale message is very attractive to every one to let this advertisement audience's attention to remember this brand of products or services are selling or serving in market at this moment. So, it is advertisement image behavior influences audiences to buy the brand's any products attractively and persuasively.

3. Raising electricity consumption from electricity user individual habit

For electricity use market case example, how to analyze people's behavior in consuming electricity using a behavioral economic framework ? Electricity consumption is modeled by the means of consumer's individual useful habit, electricity price, consumer satisfaction level, willingness to invest in new technologies, social interactions, and marketing strategies by the power utility. Because electricity is necessary to every home or electric vehicle users needs or businessmen office etc. different needs every day.

Power companies supply electricity to a region's homes and industries. However, electricity needs modernization of power system companies expect to increase price. Due to competitive factor, such as other fuel resource choices, outdated kind of energy electricity supply, and renewable fuel energy source competition.

Hence, applying behavioral economic concept, I assume electricity consumers will compare to electricity and other kinds of energy choices to weigh up the costs and benefits of all alternatives, aiming to maximize their benefits, before making a decision to choose to use electricity for their house electricity demand or electric vehicle or shop or factory manufacturing etc. function of different aspects of electricity users.

For example, electricity business clients, they aim to reduce cost, such as energy expenditure, when they use any energy to manufacture their products in factories. If they feel electricity is expensive price to compare other kinds of energy power supply. When, they feel that they can not earn much beneficial advantages to use electricity to produce their products. Otherwise, if they feel other any kinds of energy supply can replace electricity to give more benefits to compare electricity energy. Then, many business electricity users will change to use other kinds of energies to consume to replace electricity power.

However, electricity can have competitive ability in electric vehicles market, if many drivers feel environment protection is more important to compare vehicles will be popular to be driven, due to many drivers don't want air pollution. They will like gas vehicles. Hence, the main attribute from the consumer side is one their habit electricity consumption behaviors, satisfaction level, energy efficient interaction with the power utility.

Consequently how to predict electricity consumer's demand. The important factor is how to let electricity users to feel power companies are changing a reasonable level to compare other similar energy supply products. When electricity users feel electricity which can bring more benefits to compare other kinds of energy products. Then, in energy supply market, if the demanding number of electricity consumers can increase more than other kinds of energy demanding number. Then, it is right time to raise electricity price to charge electricity consumers. Hence, how to persuade electricity consumers to feel that they can have more benefits to compare other kinds of energy products. It is the main successful factor to electricity power supply companies.

● Consumer confidence is as a predictor of consumption spending

Behavioral economists believe it has link between confidence and economic decisions to cause consumers to choose spending, if the consumer has confidence to believe the product is worth to use, then who will accept to buy the product to use.

Concentrated on the conceptualization of confidence and its role in mode in theories of consumption. It also concerns on whether the confidence indicators contain any information beyond economic fundamentals. The concern is whether confidence can be explained by current and past value of variables, such as income, unemployment, inflation or consumption or in other way.

Whether confidence measures have any statistical significance in predicting economic outcomes once information from the above variables is used. Economic variable factor will also influence consumer confidence to decide consumption spending, e.g. real consumption expenditures (income, wealth or interest rate).

Finally, it will identify under which circumstances confidence indicates can be a good predictor of household consumption. Hence, survey is one good measurement method to predict whether how much every household has confidence to spend to consume the brand of products to use. Why is survey a good confidence consumption measurement prediction to every household in every country?

The reasons include survey can gather every household consumption habit history data to evaluate whether every survey person has how much confidence to consume the brand of products. Which in most cases correspond to periods where there are large changes in household survey indicators, liking during financial crises or geopolitical tensions to measure or predict whether the country's future good or bad economic condition factor will influence every household consumption desire in the year.

This modelling approach assumes that there is a certain (unknown) in confidence index changes beyond which confidence starts impacting consumption behaviors. So, sample household surveys can show the contribution of confidence in explaining consumption expenditures increases when household survey indicators feature large changes. So that confidence indicators can have some increasing predictive power during the survey investigation period in the year.

Other view point, surveys have been concerned on whether the confidence indicators contain any information beyond economic fundaments. The concern is whether confidence can be explained by current and past values of variables, such as income, unemployment, inflation or consumption or the other way. Whether confidence measures have any statistical significance in predicting economic outcomes once information from different external variable factors to influence the survey household group.

What is confidence in consumption survey ?

Confidence in consumption. For example, to measure whether how much degree of strong inflation in the economy, such as recessions and recoveries will influence the country's household confident consumption in the year.

The surveys consumers' questions usually concern on major expenditures and changes in the respondent's financial situation, focus on job availability and current business conditions etc. questions. It is then possible that about consumer confidence depending on the relative performance of the variables that may be more relevant balances, with respect to the factors that determine unemployment and other labor market related issues. It aims to investigate whether those any one of variable factors will influence consumers general loss confident consumption desire in this year.

What is a confidence indicator ?

A confidence indicator is considered as an explanatory variable for consumption together with standard variables used on predicting consumption expenditure. However, the natural real personal consumption expenditure is unexpected and unpredicted easily.

In conclusion, consumption expenditure depends the consumer individual confidence. If the consumer has much confidence to feel this year economic change will be better and he/she is easily to find job, then he/she will accept consumption easily in this year. It seems financial wealth and unemployment etc. economic factors will influence every household consumption desire. So, survey is one kind of good psychological consumption prediction method to predict consumption spending for any country in the year. I recommend manufacturers may choose to apply survey method to attempt to enquire sample survey people to gather data to predict whether what degree of consumption desire to them and find solution methods to solve low degree of consumption desire challenge.

How to apply behavioral economy methods to influence employee individual psychology to achieve raise productivity of long term incentive intention?

Increasing salary is short term incentive productivity method. Behavioral economy assumes labors will choose to do beneficial behaviors to themselves when they feel their work behaviors can earn more benefits to themselves more than their employers in the organizations. Otherwise, if they feel their work behaviors can earn more benefits to their employers more than themselves. Then, they won't choose to do their work behaviors, e.g. raising productivities or work hard. Due to they feel work hard or raise productivities behaviors that only give more benefits to their employers more themselves.

Whether does cheap product price incentive consumption desire to influence effective consumption behavior? Whether is monetary increasing salary payment incentive labors might be willing to work on task? I feel raising labors productivities is similar to raise incentive consumption, which both have similar point, such as increasing salary payment or cheap product price is the main factor to influence incentive consumption or raising productivities. Hence, it seems monetary factor is not the main effort to encourage labors to work hard.

In labor's behavioral economic view point, for example, if an employer pays an employee more doing a task, who might be less willing to work on it, who might be less productive given whose efforts and who may enjoy the task less. If you want your employees to save more for retirement. You may want to give them fewer investment options. If you want them to engage more in a task, you might want offer them an additional alternative, instead of increasing salary to that task. Thus, increasing salary is not only method to encourage productivities of incentives.

How to improve the design of incentive structures to encourage productivities in any organizations?

Any monetary incentive can only encourage productivities in short term. It can not only encourage productivities in long term in any organizations. It is similar to cheap or discount product price can only attractive consumers to buy the product in short term, it can not attract consumers to choose to buy the product in long term, it prefers to have more options to encourage labors to incentive productivities, e.g. investing good beneficial retirement plans. Suggesting that employees do not have free disposal of their investment options. These standard incentives seem irrelevant raising salary monetary factor, they can be quite effective in inducing labors to take particular actions to incentive productivities in long term. Due to when they can hard work, then they have more beneficial retirement plans or investing plans for their retirement. It means when they can achieve the most effective or efficient productivities to the employer for long term. It will give better retirement benefits and investment benefits to the better or even the best performance of employees. Otherwise, the worst performance employees won't earn good retirement benefits and investment benefits, when their employers feel their perform very poor in the organizations in long term.

Hence, increasing salary level method is not one successful long term incentive method to persuade every employee to raise productivities or encourage excellent performance optional method. Increasing salary level is only similar to reduce product price and it is only short term encouragement to consumption or productivities method.

In conclusion, extrinsic monetary factor can not incentive labor's raising productivities more than every employee themselves intrinsic motivation to raise productivities as excellent performance in any organizations. Thus, organizations need to let employees to feel that they can give long term economic benefits to encourage their intrinsic motivation effort to be raised their productivities or performance more effective or efficient in order to achieve long term both win-win economic benefits to employees and employers both.

Building employees and managers kindly co-operational relationship method

If you are an economist, your employer has no without any financial incentive to encourage your economic research tasks in your organization. It is equally difficult to certify that such activity will contribute to your growth of human capital and increased productivity in research or teaching. The standard model, which explains employee's effort only through the way (determined by productivity), is therefore incomplete. In particular, it doesn't consider that incentives to work do not have to be monetary in other words, that there are other things besides the disutility of labor (Kamenica, 2012) and section 1.3 have.

Why will short term wage increasing method only influence short term labor supply to raise productivities? The effect of reference raising wage can be most easily identified on short term labor supply to raise productivities. For US, New York city taxi drivers case, they have to decide every day for low long they are going to offer their services, given the day-to-day variable ability of demand they face (peaking during bad weather and/or when big conferences and public events are taking place in the city).

In the standard model, houses worked should grow with any growth in demand for New York taxi drivers' services. (one day's earning will have only a negligible income effect in the longer run). And yet actual cabbies work less on a demand heavy day. One of possible explanations suggests that New York city taxi drivers expect a certain income, they have set themselves a specific target income, who expect to achieve every day. During low demand for their taxi services, then they work longer hours to reach the target, when during peak demand, their referential income is achieved quickly and they only work short hours. Elasticity of hours worked with respect to their earnings is therefore negative (Lamerer, Babcock, Loewenstein, & Thaler, 1997).

However, taxi driver is either one self employment business or one taxi company employment driving service occupation. It is similar to other kinds of service jobs in societies. Servicing employees, such as waiters, salespeople, securities, customer services, bus drivers etc. different kinds of service occupations. They are not similar to manufacturing occupation to be applied how many amount of piece of products production to evaluate their productivities efforts. Thus these any one of service job nature is depended on their service performance to clients to feel their service performances are excellent to compare general service performance effort of service employees.

Considerably, respectively, I assume that if these service employees' managers can build kindly working environment, e.g. manager individual attitude and behavior can let their employees to feel happy to work together in their teams. Then, the managers' kindly as enthusiastic behaviors or attitudes will let every employee more positive encouragement of service attitude to serve their clients in their teams. Then, the client complaining number will be possible reduced, even none of any complains. Hence, building kindly relationship between managers and employees will raise excellent service performance to any organization service nature employees.

Can bonus method encourage service performance to be raised ?

In service job nature of bonus method can also raise employees' overall productivities or service performance. For example, when employees got a provisional bonus before the start of the workweek, but were warned that they would lose it on payday, unless they achieve the productivities or excellent service performance norm, they worked more productivities or let many clients to satisfy their service performance. Hence, managers can achieve bonus plan to compensate any excellent productivity or excellent services to them. Then, they can let clients to feel their service performance more satisfactory than employees of a control group who were merely given the standard promise to receive a bonus upon achieving the norm.

The effort was relatively small, however, productivity grew 1%. Interestingly, the effect of a loss was stronger when how teams were rewarded this way, social pressure came to bear on the less productivity team members. When the team members won't earn any bonus. So, long-term productivity gains were achieved through bonuses paid by excellent performance compensation method to compare to low service performance employees receiving no bonuses at all.

Economic views of human motivation nature

There are only two main types of economic actors and by making simplifying assumptions about how these types of actors behave and interact. The two basic sets of actors in this model are firms, which are assumed in this model are firms, which are assumed to maximize their profits from producing and selling products and services, households, which are assumed to maximize their utility (or satisfaction) from consuming products and services.

It seems any employees will choose to do behaviors to achieve to earn much benefits from their organizations. The models of economic behaviors that consider considerate employees' choice of goals, the actions they take to achieve these goals and the limitations and influences that affect their choices and actions.

For university students choose which universities to study case, suppose that any college enrollment students are deciding which courses to study. Thus, it implies that if the university can provide many different kinds of suitable or right courses to any college enrollment students to choose to study. It means that if the university can provide many different kinds of courses to enrollment students to choose to study. Then, it will have much chance to attract enrollment students to choose this university to study. It's competition can be raised by many courses choice factor. but, in fact, it is not absolute right, although the university can provide many courses to provide to enrollment students to choose to study. But, it is not guarantee to represent it must attract many students to enroll this university to study.

For example, suppose that college enrollment students are deciding which courses to choose to study. Although, it has right course to prepare to these enrollment students to choose to study. But, they see a summary of evaluations from hundreds of other students indicating that a certain course is very good in this university. Then, suppose that they match a video interview of just one student to give a negative review of this university of the course. Even when students were told in advance that such a negative review was worse to this university of the course. They tended to be more influenced by the negative review than the summary of hundreds of evaluations, even although such behavior seems irrational. Hence, although many right courses choice has much chance to attract students to enroll this university to study. But, if its bad educational quality from this course from negative review factor, which will influence the enrollment students number to be reduced.

It implies that students will compare this university's the course educational quality whether is better or worse to compare other universities' similar course educational quality, even this university's this course fee whether is reasonable in educational market. This is cost and beneficial comparison behavioral economy principle to all enrollment students before they decide to choose which universities.

Hence, this case implies that universities how to train teachers' teaching skills to let students to feel that they can learn new knowledge from their teaching staffs absolutely. It means how to raise education training skills to raise teachers' teaching performance. It is very important factor to influence the university's teaching development success. So, many courses choice is not important factor to attract many students to enroll the university. Otherwise, although the university can not provide many courses to let students to enroll, but it's teachers can provide excellent teaching service to teach whose students. This is important factor to attract many students to choose to enroll this university to study.

Under-level productive efficiency and low-consumption desire behavioral economic influences

In behavioral economic influence view point, I feel that under-level productive efficiency is the represent low production number to the manufacturer as well as low-consumption desire is not represent less consumers demands or customers lose confidence to the product.

On the one hand, I shall apply behavioral economic method to analyze why under productive efficiency is not represent low production number influence. Otherwise, I feel under-productive efficiency will have possible to increase production number after the manufacturer can review what factor(s) to influence under-productive efficiency.

I shall give reasons to explain as below:

As Jim, P. & Brendan. M. (2013) indicated who had ever been experiencing failure to do their businesses. Although, they had lost a million dollars, but they felt that they can be taught to learn undiscovered knowledge to know how to do their businesses successful by their wrong judgement and decision learning experience. They explained that " in ll risk taking, speculation, business ventures, entrepreneurial activities, it is the loss side on which you must focus first. This is even true for gambling, the gambler determines how much he's willing to bet, and loss, before the game is played. He doesn't wait for the game to end and then let the croupier or dealer assign his wager for him. How do you determine the downside, and how do you control or minimize it? With objective decision making and a plan that has as its starting point the stop-loss parameters"

Hence, it explains any business will have under-level productive efficiencies and low consumption desire business risk. However, to any one entrepreneur, who needs to know it is one game between the himself/herself and whose clients. They also need to know with objective decision making and a plan that has as its starting point.

Hence, I assume that if the entrepreneur has wrong decision to cause under-level productive efficiency, it is possible that, due to there is no enough employee number to manufacture the product or many employees are not skillful to manufacture all product in normal time or many employees are lazy etc. different factors to cause under-level productivities. However, when they discover their productivities are very low to compare similar competitors their employees' productivities and efficiencies. Then, they can attempt to find what factor(s) to cause low productivities and low efficiencies. it is possible that any one among of these factors case. They include many employees' lazy to influence low productivities or there is no enough employee number or many employees are not skillful to manufacture their products in production process.

Hence, wrong decision or plan is not represent failure. Otherwise, it can give chance to let the entrepreneur to learn whether what the factor(s) is (are) to cause low productivities and low efficiencies in whose product manufacturing process. As I feel that under-level productive efficiency is not represent low production number. Because I assume that if one worker lacks enough skills and manufacturing experiences to manufacture the product, but who can spend less time to manufacture the product and whose spending manufacturing time is same to the another owning enough skillful worker's time to do the product. Hence, I believe that the product quality from the low-skillful worker's manufacturing skill, it's quality will be worse to compare to the product quality from the high skillful worker's manufacturing skill. Hence, if the low skillful worker needs to spend much time to produce the product, but the product quality can be same to the high skillful worker's product quality. It means that it is sure because the low skillful worker has no excellent skill to compare to the high skillful worker to produce the product. Hence, his manufacturing spending time must be longer than the high skillful worker's time. It implies that the low skillful worker spends less time to raises high production number, but his product must be poor quality to sell. Then, his fast and efficient manufacturing speed that is not achieve economic beneficial to the organization's manufacturing process, e.g. less electricity spends to manufacture the product. Otherwise, the low skillful worker's fast and efficient manufacturing speed of behavior will raise the organization's cost in manufacturing process because consumers would not like to choose to buy any low quality product when they can choose which similar products to compare which one has the best quality and cheap price to buy.

Hence, efficient production is not the main factor to influence the business's success. Otherwise, good quality of the product factor is more important to compare it to influence the business's success.

On the other hand, I shall apply behavioral economic theory to analyze why low-consumption desire is not represent consumer demand lose to the business. As Jim. P. & Brendan. M. (2013) also identified " rather than looking for success to follow, who explained the formula for failure to avoid. As an Wang, founder of Wang laboratories said " it is my belief that there are no secret to success." The formula for failure is not lack of knowledge, brains, skills or hard work and it's not lack of luck, it's personalizing losses, especially of preceded by a string of wins or profits. It's refusing to acknowledge and accept the reality of a loss when it starts to occur because to so so would reflect negatively on you."

Thus, as whose feeling to explain why low-consumption desire is not represent less consumers demands or customers lose confidence to the product. The reasons include the causes of low-consumption desire are possible due to worse economic environment factor influences consumption desire to be reduced. It is not due to whether the product price is too high or quality is worse to compare others. Hence, as Jim & Brendan indicated the formula for business failure is not lack of knowledge, brains, skills or hard work and it's not lack of luck. It's not lack of luck. It's personalizing losses, means its reflecting to knowledge and accept the reality of a loss when it starts to occur. As it is applied to explain why low-consumption desire is not represent less consumers demands or customers lose confidence to the product. It's possible that external economic environment changing worse factor to cause the business personalizing losses, it is not reflect who lacks knowledge, skill, hard work factors to cause failure. Hence, ho to predict when and how and why economic environment changes worse will be important factor to predict when and how and why consumption behavioral changes to cause business's success.

● Demand and supply theory solves organizational problems

Any organizations can let salespeople feel happy to sell their products. Then their sale performance will also raise. The question concerns that how to make them to feel happy to help the organization to sell their products? I shall explain some methods as below:

How to manage sales for predictable revenue? In order to hold salespeople sale psychology whether they feel happy or unhappy, executives need to understand the essential activities, sales managers must focus on to be analysts for change, foster continuous improvement and create a sales culture that drives results. Sale executives need to know how to achieve top objectives of sales management is to drive sales, capture new revenue and exceed monthly sales and margin objectives, e.g. performing sale straregy development with each salesperson on Monday morning at a minimum, and in a formal one-on-one meeting during the week;using strategy tools and questioning techniques to ensure the prospects are qualified and the strategy is valid; knowing the ratio between future values and future monthly quotos to raise sale opportunities; six month on-going sale plan aims to make sure there are coordinated to achieve sale to various market segments; developing on ongoing series of networking events to build market awareness in order to ensure all salespeople attend specific events involved in networking by salespeople to, understanding the market how to influence salespeople sale method to sale number, understanding trends and seeking some channels to raise additional sales opportunities; how to create trained or warm sale environment to let sales teams feel happy to sell.

How to design and utilize efficient control sale procedures? The sale cycle procedure may include these market activities, such as
advertising, sales promotion, market research, physical distribution, pricing
, sale place, sale staffs seeking. SO, any organizations need
have good sale planning, direction and control of the personnel, selling activities of a business with including recruiting, selecting,
training, rating, supervising, paying or reward system, motivating strategy , as all these tasks apply to the personnel sales-force.
The factors may influence salespeople psychology, they may include fair income reward system, or appreciation methods and sale career development plan to every salesperson. It aims to encourage them to achieve the highest sale effort. Anymore, methods to train sale managers have the right direction to guide, lead and motivate their salespeople, e.g.

knowledge of salespeople psychology needs how to satisfy them, understanding why they choose to do or act themselves sale behaviors in order to improve their weakness to motivate salespeople to achieve company's sale target goal every month easily, e.g. raising profitability, sales volume, market share, growth and corporate image building raise clients' confidence to choose to buy this company's any products more easily.

The sales organization is required for the following purposes, they may include: enabling top-management, to devote to more time in
policy making for the growth and expansion of business to divide and fix authority among the subordinates , so that they may shirk work, to
avoid repetition of duties and functions, so that there may not be any confusion among them to locate responsibility of each and every employee , so that they can complete the whole work in stipulated time, if not then the particular person must be responsible, to establish the sales effort to enforce proper supervision of sales force.

What does the concept of salespeople replacement value mean? What is a sales force turnover management tool? Sales force turnover is defined as the rate at which salespeople leave an organizations, resignations, retirements or dismissals. So, if the organization can raise the sales force turnover ratio, because many salespeople can be promoted or the retirement, or the sales force turnover ratio raising reasons as well as they are not resignation or dismissal reasons. I believe that the organization ought have good sale environment and reasonable reward and welfare strategy to let its salespeople feel happy to help this company to sell its products every day.

However, sales management's actions have direct or indirect effects to impact on turnover. Direct effects may include the firm's firing or dismiss policy. The indirect effects on sale turnover may include new salesperon recruiting and selecting policies affect the quality and performance of the sale force as well as the speed at which salespeople are replaced. The same policies have an impact on the sales force turnover rate through the characteristics of the newly recurited salespersons and the promotion , training, retraining policies, support, supervision, compensation. ALl of those factors have an impact on salesperson's personal satisfaction or dissatisfaction absolutely. So, any sale organizations need to concern how and why whether any one of above these factors may influence their salespeople how to perform or act sale behaviors in order to excite their sale number more effective in long term.

How to achieve sale force management effectively? Sale management is one strategy to many organizations, because organizations expect their salespeople can only raise product sale number. So , they will consider whetther how to implement the sale management strategy to be the most suitable to themselves sale organizations in order to excite their sale teams to sell their products to achieve sale growth aim effectively. So for organization's long term sale growth development, it seems that one excellent sale management strategy can help the organization has stable sale number growth in long term possible.

However, the term " selling" includes a variety of sales situations and activities. For example, those sales positions where the sales representative is required primarily to deliver the product to the customer on a regular or periodic basis. The emphasis is this type of sales activity is very different to the sales position where the sales representative is dealing with sales of capital equipment to industrial purchasers. IN additions some sales representatives deal only in export markets whereas others sell direct to customers in their homes. So, sale organizations need to sell to local or overseas market as well as its target customer is businessmen or individual consumer or both in order to implement to choose their most suitable sale management strategy to train their salespeople more effective or achieving sale growth objective only. Because these its sale major target and where sale market place both factors will influence how it ought train its salespeople, so any organization's training method ought be influenced to change by whom is its major sale target and
where is its major sale market location factors.

How to know the psychology of salesmanship? WHen the organization can predict or find reasons to explain why its salespeople feel unhappy to help
this organization to sell its products. Then, it can attempt to improve its weaknesses in order to let its salespeople to feel more sale service satisfactory feeling to continue to help this organization to sell its products. THen, it won't need not often to train or recruit new salespeople to replace its old salespeople in consequence. How to know what its salespeoples' real need in order to raise their sale service satisfactory feeling ?

Psychology means that " science of the mind" and psychology plays to important part in business and it is quite worth to bring to influence any organization salespeoples' posivitive or negative sale emotion in their every sale process between themselves and their every client in personal. For example, if the salesperson often have negative emotion or he feels unhappy in every sale process, then he will encounter or increase many times of sale failure possibilities. He will feel that he is one poor verbal advertiser or seller or promotor to help his organization to promote its products to sell again as well as he will lose confidence to sell any products next sale chance, because his failure sale experiences are accumulated to influence his sale emotion to be poor or difficult sale.

Hence, the poor performance salesperson needs have more successful sale experiences to compensate his / her prior many sale failure times feeling, if the organization hopes this poor performance salesperson can raise sale number easily. Overall, any organizations need to concern how to improve or raise the more failure times of sale experience salespeoples' sale techniques or methods or attitudes more than choose to fire or dismiss them as well as finding another new salesperson to replace him/her. Because it is possible that the salesperson 's poor sale performance that is not due to himself/herself poor sale effort and sale knowledge or lacking sale experience to the product, it may be due to the poor sale team cooperation relationship , feeling poor or not comfortable sale physcial shop environment, poor sale manager and other salespeople working relationship, the sale manager lacks leadership effort, poor family relationship etc. external factors more than himself/herself personal poor or negative emotion or poor health etc. personal factors. Hence, the organization ought enquire him/her why he/she feels unhappy to sell its products and it needs to attempt to find methods to solve his/her challenges immediately. If his/her challenges can be solved. It is possible that his/her sale efforts can be also raised for. So, if the organization can know how to utilize positive sale emotion psychological methods to predict or know why and how every salesperson perform his/her sale behavior in whose daily sale tasks, then it can concentrate on implementing effective and the most suitable sale training to raise their sale abilities more easily.

However, the sale training may include: How to build or improve long term good salesperson and his/her customer sale service relationship between every salesperson and every client in every buying and selling cycle process, how to using right communicating styleds for better understanding every client's real needs, powers and negotiating, e.g. every salesperson needs to review why there are many clients do not choose to buy any products from his sale presentation or promotion, finding every time sale failure reasons can let the salesperson makes himself/herself sale failure reasons evaluation or judgement in order to find what is the major reason influences his/her sale failure, e.g. lacking product knowledge, he/she often let many clients to feel that he lacks patience to listen the client's enquiry or feedback, his sale presentation is not attractive to let many clients like to stay longer time to listen his sale presentation in whole sale process, the salesperson himself/herself emotion is negative and he /she can let many clients feel he / she is not happy or does not enjoy to sell this product from himself/herself face impression or sale behavior impression easily, lacking enough sale techniques to persuade his/her clients why he/she ought choose to buy this product in whole sale process etc. these factors may influence the salesperson's sale failure chance to be raised. Hence sales manager ought need to spend long time to meet the poor sale performance salesperson to discuess what his/her sale challenges are the most major to influence his/her every sale successful chance in order to improve his/ her sale performance more successfully.

IN conclusion, the reasons why salespeople often encounter sale failure possibilities. The factors may include these aspects, such as they lask the desire to help customers to make satisfactory purchase decisons, they only concern how to achieve sale final objective or aim only, it will cause clients feel they do not real concern their real needs. They only concern to sell the product in success. They do not know how to describe the product whether what characteristics or features it owns accurately in order to increase sale chance to persudade them to make final decision to by the product, they do not attempt to participate the whole sale process to help them to choose the most right product in order to satisfy their any purcahse needs, they ought avoid deceptive or manipulative influence tactics, avoid the use of high pressure sales techniques etc. Thus, if any organizations can spend time to investigate what factors cause why any one of salespeople choose perform his/her sale behavior often in order to know or understand their salespeople' sale psychology absolutely. Then, I believe that their sale number will only grown more easily.

CHAPTER TWO

(AI) -driven automation industry demand and supply market analysis

● (AI) - driven automation industry demand and supply market to need

(AI) -driven automation industry will create wealth and expand economy growth to any countries, but it will be accompanied by changed in the skills that workers need to learn. One of main ways that technology increases productivity is by decreasing the number of labor hours needed to create a unit of output. It implies (AI) technology will influence low educated and low skillful labor number to be decreased (reduction employment number).

Whether how to demand robotic products in manufacturing and service markets as well as how it will bring supply to be suitable distribution to different kinds of manufacturing and serivce industries needs, e.g. non -manual driven vehicle, non-manual driven air plane, ship, warehouse robotics, shopping center artificial intelligent service robotics? Whether do robotic needs to service industry more or manufacturing industry more?

In contrast, technological change tended to work in a different direction throughout the nowadays. The advance of computer and the internet raised the relative productivity of higher skilled workers. So, routine-intensive occupations that focused on predictable tasks disappearance, such as switch board, operators, filming checkers, travel agents and assembling line workers etc. were particularly replaced by new technologies.

However, today, it may be challenging to predict exactly which jobs , such as service industry, shopping center robotic, or manufacturing industry, warehouse robotic manufacturing workers etc. which will be most immediately affected by (AI) driven-automation in demand and supply view. The reason is because (AI) is not a single technology, but rather a collection of technologies that are felt unevenly through the economy to influence job changing both negatively and positively. In positively view point, (AI) driven-automation will make many workers more productive and increase demand for certain skills. Consequently, new jobs are likely to be directly create in areas , such as the development and supervision of (AI) as well as indirectly created in a range of areas throughout the economy as higher incomes lead to expanded demand. Otherwise, in negatively view point, many traditional human needed (demand) skillful jobs will be threatened by automation are highly concentrated among lower-paid, lower-skilled and less -educated workers. It means automation will cause pressure on demand for this group, pressure and employment, if (AI) can replace the low skilled and less educated workers' jobs. Thus, (AI) will have negative influence to impact on the labor market.

(AI) capabilities will enable automation of some tasks that have long required human labor in service industry more or manufacturing industry more. Can (AI) replace some simple human jobs to service tasks or manufacturing tasks more? For example, advances in robotics are expanding machines' abilities to interact with and sharp the physical world. Combined , (AI) and robotics will give rise to smarter machines that can perform more sophisticated functions than ever before and brings more advantages that humans have exercised. This will permit automation of many tasks now performed by human workers and could change the shape of the labor market and human activity. So, we need to analyze whether (AI) roboic can help human to do whether tasks on service industry more or manufacturing tasks more. Then, we can evaluate whether our service industry will need robotics more or manufacturing industry more.

● How (AI) influences labor market change on service and manufacturing industries aspect

Today, it may be challenging to predict exactly which jobs will be most immediately affected by (AI)-driven automation. Because (AI) is not a single technology, but rather a collection of technologies that are applied to specific tasks. So, deciding whether future service or manufacturing tasks needs on robotics replacing manual tasks aspect more. They need to depend on whether either future many service simple tasks can be replaced by robotic to do more or future many manufacturing tasks can be replaced by robotic to do more. So, we ought need to consider whether many manual tasks can be replaced to do by robotics or whhether many manual tasks can be replaced by robotics to do more in demand and supply view. Then, robotic manufacturers can decide whether they ought invent more robotics on service industry aspect or they ought invent more robotics on manufacturing industry aspect in this robotic manufacturing supply and demand market.

Some specific future robotic service industry or manufacturing demand and supply need predictions are possible based on the current (AI) technology invention effort whether the robotics scientists can have enough technology to manufacture any kinds of robotic products on service tasks or manufacturing tasks aspects. For example, driving jobs and house cleaning jobs, bank counter service jobs, telephone enquiry service operators. Restaurant cooking jobs, simple accounting record service jobs etc. that require relatively less education to perform. Advancements in computer vision and related technologies have made the feasibility of fully appear more likely, potentially displacing some workers in driving-dominant professions. Seemingly similar robot, for which the operational tasks is less specific of navigating to a specific destination when following a set of given rules and preserving safety. But, I believe that robotic scientists ought not follow their robotic manufacturing technology to decide whether they ought manufacture robotic service machines more or robotic manufacturing machines more in future robotic supply market. Because their technology can not represent that future human will need more robotic supply on either service industry more or manufacturing industry more. Future whether what human tasks are more popular to be replaced by robotics. They are depended on whether what kinds of service tasks can be simple to replaced by robotics more or whether what kinds of manufacturing tasks can be simple to replaced by robotic more factor , it means that how many simple manual service tasks or simple manual manufacturing tasks can be replaced by robotic.

In the future, the effects of (AI) on the labor market in the decade ahead will continue the trend toward skill-biased change that computerization and communication innovations have driven in recent decades. Thus, some human driving occupation will be disappeared or replaced by (AI) automation driven. For example, bus drivers, light truck or delivery services drivers, heavy and tractor-trailer truck drivers, school drivers, tax drivers, travel bus drivers. These will be future robotics needs on public transport service industry.

However, (AI) technology could enable some workers to focus time on other job responsibilities, boosting their productivity, and actually raised wage growth among those still holding the reshaped jobs. For example, salespeople, who currently spend a considerable amount of time driving could find themselves able to do other work when a car drives them from place to place, or inspectors and appraisers could fill out paperwork, when their car drives itself. This (AI) -driven technology should make these workers more productive, with (AI) -driven technology serving as a complement, not a substitute. New jobs will also likely be created, both in existing occupations cheaper transportation costs with lower prices and increase demand for products and all the related occupations, such as service and fulfillment, and in new occupations not currently foreseeable. These are other kinds of transport part service tasks needs on robotics.

What kind of jobs will be created by (AI) technology in whole job process on service or manufacturing industry? Predicting future job growth is extremely difficult, due to it depends on technologies or substitute for existing today as well as they may complement or substitute for existing human skills and jobs. However, (AI) will also lead to substantial indirect job creation to the degree it raises productivity and wages, it may also lead to higher consumption that would support additional jobs from high-end draft production to restaurant and retail. The future(AI) " augmented intelligence", the technology's role is as assisting and expanding the productivity of individuals rather than replacing human work. Thus, based on the biased-technical change framework, demand for labor will likely increase the most in the areas where humans complement (AI) automation technologies. For example, (AI) technology , such as IBM's Watson may improve early detection of some cancers or other illnesses, but a human healthcare professional is needed to work with patients to understand and translate patients' symptoms, inform patients of treatment options, and guide patients through treatment plans. Shipping companies may also partner workers who pick up and deliver products over the last feet with (AI) enabled autonomous vehicles that move workers efficiently from site to site. In such cases, (AI) augments what a human is able to do and allows individuals to either be move effective in their specially task or to operate on a larger scale. Thus, it seems (AI) technology will also create new jobs, raise productivities and workers' efficiencies on future factory warehouse delivery tasks.

● Redefining management in the workforce of artificial intelligent clerical tasks need office industry

In the future, due to artificial intelligence influences to some kind of human jobs nature in office administrative productive tasks environment in order to help any offices to raise administrative efficiencies by robotics. So, the kind of human jobs of management methods will also need to change to adapt the artificial intelligence technology input to their organizations. It will cause challenges for every executive and manager if who won't have effort to manage their teams how to apply artificial intelligence technology to work efficiently and easily. For example, division of labor will change among humans and machines will increase. Thus, companies will have to adapt their training performance and talent strategies how to emphasize on work that how to make human judgment and skills and experimentation. Thus, (IA)'s greatest impact will be on administrative coordination and control tasks, such as scheduling , resource allocation.

In fact, mangers will encounter this challenges: How to apply human experience and expertise to judge critical business decisions and practices when the information available is insufficient to suggest a successful course of action? Due to this kind of work will require new skills and mindsets. I shall indicate these change management methods to adapt (AI) technology. Such as: administration and routine tasks, scheduling , allocation of resources and reporting will fall within the intelligence machines, responsibilities that have long been reserved for humans. For example, a typical store manager or a lead nurse at a nursing home most constantly arrange shift schedules, accounting for staff members' absences owing to illness, vacation time or sudden departures.

Thus, the managers need to learn how to arrange new division of labor within the organizations after (AI) technology had been implemented to the organization. Artificial intelligence is currently influencing into once considered exclusive to humans: assessing and acting on human emotions and personality traits. The influences to managers need to change their strategies to adapt (AI) technology implements include such as below:

Firstly, managers need to spend the bulk of their time on coordination and control tasks from intelligent system implements. Their time spending on these major three aspects from impact of intelligent system: coordinate and control, solve problems and collaborate and people and community , strategy and innovation three aspects. Thus (AI) will influence managers need to change their judgment method to teach whose teams how to adapt the (AI) system operations in any organizations.

Secondly, (AI) will influence top, middle and low level management needs to change to adapt the (AI) technology operations to any owned (AI) technology organizations in the future. Intelligent machines must be trained in context. Just like humans , on-the-job training is a requirement for such machines because they typically arrive with only very general capabilities. To get the most from (AI), managers at all levels must participate in the instructional experience and in the learning process and provides managers' familiarity with such systems on these aspects, e.g. How the system works and generate advice, how the system has a proven track record , how the system provides convincing explanations , how the system can make simple rule- based decisions.

Thirdly, managers need to learn how to make judgment more accurate (AI) systems assistance. Although (AI) will invariably take on more routine work and even augment human decision-making, it won't judgment work, the application of human experience and expertise to critical business decisions when the information available is insufficient to suggest a successful course of action or reliable enough to suggest an obvious course of action. For a sense of the nature of judgment work, consider big data marketing and sales analytics. Such analytics often provide insights that can inform promotional campaigns, including predicting which promotions will generate desired sales brand further into the future, marketing executives need use judgment, combining analytics with their own and others' insight and experience.

The application of experience and expertise to critical business decisions and practice represents the real value of human judgment. But, when artificial intelligent machines are implemented to any organizations to assist the low, middle and top level management to make any business judgment. These forms of judgment work that managers can gather data interpretation, idea development more absolute from (AI) machine assistance. Thus, why these level management executives need to learn how to apply (AI) machines to help them to make any business judgment more accurate. Future offices will need robotics to help their some staffs to do simple administrative tasks.

● (AI) influences organizational change to help senior management to do strategic decision tasks in office environment

Consequently creative and social intelligence will be in even greater demand as (AI) makes in management and the workforce. This development will represent a long term trend in labor markets , one characterized by intensifying demand and reward for social skills with a growing desire for creative capabilities, managers will seek to fashion of ideas and hypotheses from inside and outside of the enterprise to shape solutions to their most pressing business problems. Thus, (AI) will influence overall organizational team members who have chance to participate any decision to make more accurate business judgment.

Many managers mistakenly view judgment work as only an individual discipline, failing to appreciate that it can also involve decide interpersonal and organizational practices. In more complex settings, judgment is typically a collective outcome of individuals' and teams' diverse perspectives, insights and experiences. And often , the resulting choices are better informed than decisions that an individual would have arrived at on his or her own.

Thus, when any organizations apply (AI) technology to assist managers to gather data and ideas to make any judgment. In these cases, organizations can create the conditions for effective collective judgment by establishing structures , such as " shadow advisory boards" that prompt managers and employees to source and synthesize multiple perspectives. Thus, a traditional organization (firm) might freshen its thinking is t put together a shadow advisory board, comprised of young, digital people who can apply (AI) machine assistance to make judgment work more accurate whether related to people development, problem-solving or strategizing and innovating for considerable degrees of creative and social intelligence.

Thus, on the one hand, (AI) technology machine augmentation and automation can give these advantages to human (organization managers) , e.g. developing people and community, solving problems and collaborating, coordinating and controlling work, shaping strategy and leading innovation. Besides, on the other hand, the next generation managers need have these individual attitude to treat intelligent machines to be as colleagues.

When, judgment is a human skill, intelligent machines can accelerate human learning that supports it, assisting in data -driven simulations, scenarios and search and discovery activities. Focuses on judgment work, some decisions require insight beyond what data can tell them. This is the sweet sport for human judgment, the application of experience and expertise to critical business decisions and practices. Thus, managers will also need to find ways to learn how to use digital (AI) technologies to tap into the knowledge and judgment of partners, customer external stakeholders and role models in other industries after the (AI) machine had been implemented to the organization. Future robotics will have more needs on senior management strategic decision aspect in office environment.

● Future works change: Automation, employment
and productivity on sevice and manufacturing industries by service robotics and manufacturing robotics both

● How (AI) influences future service and manufacturing industries job change

Human future " micro to macro" industry trends will be affected business strategy and public policy by (AI) technology. In the future (AI) technology will influence those six themes: productivity and growth, natural resources, labor markets, the evolution of global financial markets, the economic impact of technology and innovation and urbanization. However, (AI) technology will bring economic benefits of tackling gender inequality, a new global competition, Chinese innovation and digital globalization.

Nowadays, advances in robotics artificial intelligence, and machine learning are in a new age of automation, as machines match or outperform human performance in a development to any countries. For example, automation of activities can enable businesses to improve performance by reducing errors and improving quality and speed, and in some cases achieving outcomes that go beyond human capabilities. For example, some research indicated automation could raise productivity growth globally by 0.8 to 1.4 % annually; more than 2,000 work activities across 800 occupations. When less than 5% of all occupations can be automated using demonstrated technologies about 60% of all occupations have at least 30% of constituent activities that could be automated. Many occupations will change that will be automated away: Activities most susceptible to automation involve physical activities, in highly structured and predictable environments, as well as the collection and processing of data. They are most prevalent in manufacturing , accommodation and food service and retail trade and include some middle-skill jobs. For example, such as natural language processing is a key factor. Beyond technical feasibility, the cost of technology competition with labor including skills and supply and demand dynamics, performance benefits including and beyond labor cost savings, and social and regulatory acceptance will be affected by (AI) automation technology. Thus, (AI) automation will impact to influence global employment in those aspects as below:

Firstly, assuming that people are displaced by automation will find other employment. The anticipated shift in the activities in the labor force is of a similar order as the long-term shift away from agriculture and decreases in manufacturing share of employment. Both of manufacturing and agriculture industries which would be accompanied by the creation of new types of work not foreseen at the time.

Secondly, for business, the performance benefits of automation are relatively clear. Thus, the businessmen have opportunities for their micro economies to benefits from the productivity growth potential and macro economies to benefit to encourage continued progress and innovation , investment and market incentives. At the same time, employers must innovate policies to help workers and institutions adapt to the impact on employment.

This will likely include rethinking education and training, income support and safety nets , as well as support for those dislocated, when employees need to leave themselves homes to move to other cities to learn new (AI) automation works. Thus, individuals in the workplace will need to engage move comprehensively with machines as part of their everyday activities, and acquire new skills that will be in demand in the new automation age. Consequently , the scale of shifts in the labor force over many decades that automation technologies can be a similar order to the long -term technology -enables shifts in the developed countries' workforces away from agriculture in the 21 th century. Those shifts did not result in long-term mass unemployment because they were accompanied by the creation of new types of work not foreseen at the time. However, human will still be needed in the workforce when the total productivity gains are caused by (AI) technology.

● What occupations will be influenced by (AI) technology on future service and manufacturing tasks aspects

In the future, scientists predict that these occupations will be influenced by (AI) technology mostly. They include : retail salespeople, food and beverage service workers, language or translation teachers, health practitioners. Since these work activities have a more relevant occupations are made up of a range of activities with different potential for (AI) automation . For example, a retail salesperson will spend more time interacting with customers, stocking shelves , or ringing up sales. Each of these activities is distinct and requires different capabilities to perform successfully.

Thus, these job activities have similar simple control characteristics. Simple activities include greet customers, answer questions about products and services, clean and maintain work areas, demonstrate product feature process sales and transactions. All these activities can have similar simple activities in order to (AI) machines can be learn how to do these activities from (AI) technology . For example, the capability perception includes sensory perception, cognitive capabilities, such as retrieving automation, recognizing known patterns(supervised learning), logical reasoning problem solving.

Thus, (AI) machine is such human, which has feeling and emotion, such as social and emotional sensing, judgement reasoning methods, natural language understanding and physical capabilities, such as mobility , navigation, gross motor skill, fine motor skills. It seems that the future, (AI) human invents machines which will have these human characteristics to do human similar behavioral job duties more easily and efficiently. It implies these above human occupations will be replaced by (AI) human invention machines in the future. Due to (AI) creation, it is possible to cause unemployment number of these above workers will increase because (AI) machines can do their similar job behavioral activities.

Consequently, employers won't need to employ many of these skillful labor. Otherwise, they can buy less number (AI) machines to attempt to do whose job activities more easily and efficiently. So, it seems (AI) machines will have more high work performance to replace these occupation workers' work performance. Finally, these occupation worker unemployment number will only increase when the (AI) machines had been invented to achieve to do their work behavioral activities absolutely success in the future.

● Whether (A) technology machine labor will replace human worker more or assist human worker more

There is no single agreed definition of a robot how outcome of a task that is completed without human intervention. When some definitions require the task to be completed by a physical machine moves and respond to its environment, other definitions use the term robot in connection with tasks completed by software , without physical embodiment.

However, to answer the question : Whether (AI) technology machine labor will replace human worker more or assist human worker more. I shall indicate some examples to let readers to judge whether (AI) technology can create new jobs or reduce old jobs.

Firstly, I shall explain what (AI) function is. (AI) is a service robot that performs useful tasks for humans or equipment excluding industrial automation application . Thus, the classification of a robot into industrial robot or service robot is done according to its intended application. It is also a personal service robot or a service robot for personal used for a non commercial task, usually by lay persons . Examples are domestic servant robot, and pet exercising robot. It is also a professional service robot or a service robot for professional used for a commercial task, usually operated by a properly trained operator. Examples, are cleaning robot for public places, delivery robot in offices or hospitals, fire-fighting robot, rehabilitation robot and surgery robot in hospitals. Thus, these functions will be future (AI) application to our daily life necessaries or business necessaries.

However, some authors agree (AI) will bring negative outcomes of automation, due to raise competiveness, reduce human job nature. Otherwise, other authors argue (AI) will bring positive outcomes of automation, due to raise productivities, job creation, assist humans work.

On the positive outcome hand, robots can increase productivity . This is particularly important for small-to medium sized businesses both are in developed and developing countries economies. It also enables large companies to increase their competitiveness through faster product development and delivery. Increased use of robot is also enabling companies in high cost countries to re shore, or bring back to their domestic base parts of the supply chain that will have previously outsourced to sources of cheaper labor. Currently , the greater threat to employment is not a automation, but an inability to remain competitive. Automation has led overall to an increase in labor demand and positive impact on wages. The reason is that the middle-income/middle-skilled jobs have reduced as a proportion of overall contribution to employment and earnings leading to fears of increasing income inequality, the skills range within the middle income bracket is large. Thus, robots are driving an increase in demand for workers at the higher -skilled and with a positive impact on wages. This issue is how to enable middle-income earners in the lower-income range to unskilled or retain. Finally, the (AI) positive impact supporter who argue the future will be robots and humans can work together.

However, on the negative outcome hand, robots can substitute labor activities, but don't replace jobs. They believe that less than 10% of jobs are fully automatable. Increasingly , robots are used to complement and augment labor activities, the net impact on jobs and the quality of work is positive. Automation can provide the opportunity for humans to focus on higher-skilled, higher-quality and higher-paid tasks. Robots can improve productivity when they are applied to tasks that which perform more efficiently and to a higher and more consistent level of quality than humans. For example, increased productivity is enabling some firms, such as Whirlpool, Caterpillar and Ford Motors company in the US restructure their supply chains, bringing back parts of the manufacturing process to the country of origin. Thus, productivity gains due to robotics and automation are important not just at the company level, but also for build industry and nation competitiveness.

I suppose that productivity can be raised. What are the impacts of robots on employment? Firstly, the main focus of development has been on personal entertainment, which does not drive worker productivity (manufacturing production). When the internet (information and communication technology (ICT)) innovation. This is borne and by findings that manufacturing productivity, which has been driven by innovations in automation rather than consumer technologies, has government strongly than productivity in the services sectors of the economy in most nature economies. It seems (AI) automation will create many jobs in internet communication entertainment game industry. For example, many young people like to use internet to play any electronic games from computer or mobile at home or outside home conveniently. Thus, (AI) automation will increase demand to be invented to any new entertainment game from internet channel. It will need to employ many (AI) entertainment game inventors to create many automation entertainment games. Thus, (AI) automation in internet entertainment game industry will need human (AI) entertainment game inventors to invent the knowledge-based capital of (AI) automation entertainment games. The (AI) entertainment game inventors will need own research and development skills, form specific skills, organizational know-how skills, databased knowledge, design and various forms of intellectual property to do these (AI) automation entertainment game invention occupations in the future.

International Federation Of Robotics(2016) indicated that China will be as a major robotics manufacturer and user of robots, benefiting from jobs created by robot manufacturing and productivity gains from robot use. Chins had sold of robots to any one single market every year since 2017 year. The Chinese government has included a focus on robotics in its 10 year strategy. In order to achieve its target of a robot density of 150 units per 10, 000 workers by 2020 year. Thus, Chinese companies will have to install around 650,000 new industrial robots between 2016 to 2020 year, 2.5 times more than installed globally in 2015 year.

Hence, China (AI) manufacturing industry will need to employ many workers . It implies (AI) manufacturing industry will create many new occupations in China. Also, ministry of economy, trade and industry (2015) also showed that Japan currently has the largest stock of industrial robots in operations, primarily in the automation industry. Driven by a rapidly aging population and low productivity rates, the Japanese government has sights on a 20-fold increase in the use of robots in the non-manufacturing sector and a three-fold growth rate of labor productivity in the service sector both by 2020 year. Thus, it also implies Japan will need many robots to be provide to service industry. Due to robots will provide to serve any businessmen's clients. Thus, it is possible that the service workers won't be dismissed as well as it is depended on the serving job nature to decide whether Japan's service workers can still serve to their employer when the service (AI) robots are applied to whose employers.

Consequently, it seems that (AI) can create employment, Ministry of economy, trade and industry (2015) showed that such as China will develop the major (AI) automation manufacturing industry. The (AI) employers will need to employ many workers to manufacture any these different kinds of (AI) robots to satisfy China or overseas individual or business buyers needs. But, (AI) can also cause unemployment to the low skillful service workers. Such as if Japan some service businesses choose to buy any (AI) service robots to replace their service staffs to serve their clients. It is possible that the service staffs will be dismissed, due to (AI) robots can do such as their same service job duties to achieve better service performance. Thus, today, it is increasingly common for people to use robots in various situations at home and in retail stores, hotels and hospitals these service industries. Robots are classified into server types based on their functionality (service and utility robots or those designed to communicate with humans) and appearance (humanoid robots or mechanical robots). The type of robot, to which each country allocated particular importance in the advance of robotics, reflects the sense of values and preferences of its population. Thus, if the country has high population needs to use robots, then they will influence either more new jobs creation or more old job loss in the country's (AI) manufacturing or (AI) service industries both. For example, Japan respondents often associate the term " robot " with humanoid robots that can communicate with human and they have a high level of familiarity with robot. The US has the highest level of robot utilization at home and in retail stores with its people being the most enthusiastic about the future use of robots. Germany shows a strong tendency to consider robots for industrial purposes and its people feel strong effort to the presence of robots in their households.

In conclusion, to judge whether how (AI) will influence the country's employment to be better or worse. It will depend on the country home buyers (users) or business buyers (users) how to use (AI) for their daily needs. If the country , such as US retail stores need to use (AI) , it will have possible to reduce some or many retail service workers. Even, if the country , such as Japan has many home users need to use (AI) , it will not influence the employment market. Otherwise, it will raise (AI) salespeople numbers. Even, if the country, such as Germany and China will have many (AI) manufacturers, then it will create many (AI) manufacturing occupations for these (AI) manufactory workers.

Consequently, (AI) robots manufacturing and service needs will have positive or negative impact to any country's employment. It will depend on the (AI) service provision and service workers' job nature as well as the manufacturing workers of (AI) knowledge level to decide their employment chance in their country's employment.

● Whether robotic will bring more attribution to our future social service industry more or manufacturing industry more?

Some scientists explain that artificial intelligence means which is an expert system, computer software that embodies a portion of the specialized knowledge of a human portion in a specific, narrow domain, owns decision making ability of human expert. The (AI)technology is based on the premise that what makes a person an expert is years of experience that enables who recognizes certain patterns in a problem as being similar to pattern. For example, in the future artificial intelligence system can be applied to control air traffic, design to computer configuration, medical diagnosis, instruction/training, speech/interpretation, monitoring to (nuclear plant), planning to mission, factory scheduling, prediction weather, repairing telephone, automatic driving etc. different industries.

Artificial intelligence characteristics include: creative, adaptive , common sense, fact processing, quick replication, broad focus permanent and consistent skill. Otherwise, traditional computer expert system disadvantage includes perishable, unpredictable, slow reproduction, expensive, slow reproduction, slow processing lacks inspiration, needs instruction, narrow focus only machine knowledge. So, artificial intelligence is a branch of computer science devoted to creating computer to influence software and hardware to attempt to create human intelligence or human intelligent behavior. It is learning from experience, responds flexibility in situation that are, new or not anticipated.

Thus, (AI) can be learnt programmed knowledge to solve problems, using reasoning in solving problem, understanding and inferring facts and rules, recognizing the relative importance of different elements in a situation. In summary, artificial intelligence is concerned with two basic ideas mainly: The first idea, it involves studying the thought processes of humans to understand what intelligence is; the second idea, it deals with representing thought processes using companies to create artificially intelligent entities for testing the theories of intelligence.

● Can (AI) impact human job nature change more on service industry or manufacturing industry?

Human need concern this question: Will artificial intelligence (AI) reduce some human jobs in order to instead of replacing machines to do? Due to artificial intelligence is the ability of machines to do thing, that people would require intelligence. For example, artificial intelligence machine man driving(self-driver), it (AI) machine man driving research is an attempt to discover and describe aspects of human intelligence that can be simulated by driving machine functions. Alternatively, (AI) mathematical research may be another viewed as an attempt to develop a mathematical theory function to describe the abilities and actions of things (natural or man-made) exhibiting intelligent behavior and server as a design of intelligent calculation machine function.

Why do humans need artificial intelligence machines to instead of traditional human service job? For example, can artificial intelligence machine man (self-driving) driver drive to replace human driver? I shall compare the differences between humans and computers : The characteristics of humans are good at recognizing various things, either seen before or not, recognizing the relationship patterns between things. Human thinking is common sense reasoning, combining all types of sensory input, acting appropriately in novel situations, learning new things and changing behavior patterns, making decisions , even when given incomplete information, working with noisy, incomplete information gathering behaviors . However, characteristics of computers are good at: The tasks humans do naturally are extremely difficult for a computer program as intelligent, which must be able to do the same kind of tack as humans do naturally.

Hence, (AI) is an combination of many different success and technologies: Linguistics - computational and socio, philosophy-logic, philosophy of mind and of language, electronical engineering -image and speech processing, pattern recognition, robotics, machine learning, neural networks, optimization scheduling, management information system and decision making. So, it is possible that (AI) can impact human job nature to instead of human working behavior in the future.

How can (AI) influence labor market?
● How can human social job nature
to be changed to accept to use whole tasks steps on artificial intelligent manufacturing industry or artificial intelligent service industry?

I believe that how to decide whether robotic needs are more on manufacturing industry or service indusry. It depends on whether they are how many whole tasks steps of any service or manufacturing occupations are accepted to be replaced by robotics ? From the first intelligent perspective reason view point, artificial intelligence is making machines " intelligent" acting as humans expect people to act. Artificial intelligence has ability to distinguish computer responses from human responses, it owns knowledge to solve expert problem. From another research perspective reason view point, artificial intelligence is the study of how to make computers do things which, at the moment, people do better (Rich & Knight, 1991, p.3).

(AI) researchers are native in a variety of domains, e.g. formal tasks (mathematics, games), tasks (perception, robotics, natural language, common sense reasoning), expert tasks (financial analysis, medical diagnostics, engineering, scientific analysis and other areas).

From the second business perspective reason view point, (AI) is a set of many powerful tools, and methodologies for using those tools to solve business problems. From a programming perspective reason view point, (AI) includes the study of symbolic programming problem solving and search .

From the third human technological perspective reason view point, today's computer can do many well-defined tasks, for example, arithmetic operations, are much faster and more accurate than human beings. However, the computers' interaction with their environment is not very sophisticated yet. How can human test whether a computer has reached the general intelligence level of a human being? Can a computer convince a human interrogator that it is a human? But before thinking of such advanced kinds of machines, human will start developing our own extremely simple " intelligent" machines. So, it is possible that human society job nature will to be changed to artificial intelligent society when (AI) technology is developed to the mature stage in the future.

● Why do some service or manufacturing providers need artificial intelligence machines to replace manual service workers or manufacturing workers in our future societies?

One of major division in (AI) is between humans who think (AI) is the only serious way of finding out how we (human) work and human who want companies to do very smart things, independently of how we (human) work. This is the important distinction between cognitive scientists vs engineers. One of another major division in (AI) is between symbolic (AI), which represents information through symbols and their relationships. Specific Algorithms are used to process these symbols to solve problems or deduce new knowledge and connectionist. So (AI) , which represents information in network. Biological processes underlying learning, task performance and problem solving are imitated from human mind behaviors. Thus, it is possible that artificial intelligence machines can do the better judgicious behavior to compare human.

● How does artificial intelligence influence future working changing in automative manufacturing or automative service tasks aspects?

In the automation changing influence aspect, as companies increasingly use robots on production lines or algorithms to optimize their logistics manage inventory, any carry out other core business functions. Technological advances are creating a new automation age in which ever-smarter and more flexible machines will be deployed on an ever larger scale in the marketplace. However, researching artificial intelligence with how influences human working nature. We need to answer these questions: How will automation transform the workplace? What will the implications for employment? And what is likely to be its impact both on productivity in the global economy and on employment?

Advances in robotics, artificial intelligence, and machine learning are growing in a new age of automation as machines match or outperform human performance in a range of work activities, including ones requiring cognitive capabilities. What factors are determined the changing in workplace adoption by artificial intelligence innovation? What advantages are automation? Automation of activities can be enabled businesses to improve performance by reducing errors and improving quality and speed, and achieving outcomes that go beyond human capabilities.

Some scientists indicated based on their scenario modeling. They estimated automation could raise producing growth globally by 0.8 to 1.4 percent annually. Almost, the activities people are paid almost $16 trillion in wages to do in global economy have the potential to be automated by adopting currently demonstrated technology. According to their analysis of more than 2,000 work activities across 800 occupations. When less than 5% of all occupations have of least 30% of activities that could be automated. They also indicated that technical economic and social factors will determine automation. Continued technical progress, for example, in areas such as natural language processing is a key factor beyond technical feasibility , the cost of technology, competition with labor including skills, and supply and demand dynamics, performance benefits including and beyond labor cost savings and social and regulatory acceptance will affect (alter) the scope of automation.

Other some scientists also indicate U.S. country for example, the anticipate shift in the activities in labor force of a similar order of magnitude as the long term sight away from agriculture and decreases in manufacturing. Share of employment in the United States both which were achieved. So, those factors can influence why artificial intelligence technology needs. So, it is possible that future agriculture and manufacturing both industries will apply (AI) technology manufacturer-kind of job nature to raise productivity instead of farmers, fruit picking workers, farming transportation labours as well as factory manufacturing workers and supervisors etc. human-kind of job nature.

● Is artificial intelligence possible to replace any service occupation or manufacturing labor to finish whole tasks steps of some service or manufacturing occupations in our societies ?

Not just intelligence, but also debating, if machines are capable of having a conscious minds. Artificial intelligence has those characteristics as below:

On functionalism aspect, artificial intelligence inputs mental states, sensory inputs, (beliefs, desires being in pain feeling) and behavioral outputs. Since mental states are identified by a functional role, which are thoughts to be manifested in various systems. Even, perhaps computers which are physical devices with electronic substrate that inform computations on inputs to give outputs similar to brains which are artificial intelligence composed of part any intrinsic relationship to each other. Thus, artificial intelligence activities is not the whole itself, but into parts or on external influence on the parts.

On dualism aspect, artificial intelligence is a set of views about the relationship between mind are matter. On materialism aspect, it builds the only thing that exists is matter, including consciousness.

On biological naturalism aspect, it is similar a human brain than feels pains makes mental situation. So, artificial intelligence is similar biologist which might to be excited to human labor work. Hence, it seems artificial intelligence can change (alter) or replace human labor work of nature in possible in the future.

On technological innovation reason view point, the history development of artificial intelligence studying the intelligence is one of most ancient scientific discipline. The history development of artificial intelligence what aims to achieve human use to sense, learn remember and think, logic probability, decision making and calculation develop from mathematics, instead of replacement human labor functions.

Artificial intelligence history development aim is the scientific analysis of skills in connection and practice with the appearance of computers from 1950 year beginning. The artificial intelligence (AI) can deal with the ultimate challenges. How can (either biological or electronic) mind sense, understand and manipulate a world that is much simple and more complex than itself? And what if would human like to construct something with such capabilities?

The general-purpose software of the early period of (AI) were only able to solve simple tasks effectively and failed when which should be used in a wider range or an more difficult tasks. One of the sources of difficulty was that early software had very few or mix knowledge about the problems which handled, and activities successes by simply syntactic manipulation. Moreover, the other difficulty was that many problems that were tried to solve by the (AI) were untreatable.

The early (AI) software whether trying step sequences based on the basic facts about the problem that should be solved, experimented with different combinations till which found a solution. From the end the 1960 year, developing the so-called expert systems were emphasized. These systems had (sue-based) knowledge base about the field which handled. Till to the beginning of the 1970 year, (Prolog) the logical programming language was born, which was built in the computation realization of a version of the resolution calculus. (Prolog) is a remarkably prevalent tool in developing expert systems (on medical, judiciary and other scopes), but natural language parsers were implemented in this language. Then, in 1981 s, the Japanese announced the fifth generation computer system project, a 10 years plan to build an intelligent computer system that use the (Prolog) language as a machine code. Nowadays, (AI) can be applied any industries, such as car manufacturing industry can use (AI) technological machine-men manufacture car, instead of replacing human labors in factory. Even, in the future, using (AI) machine-men drivers can drive any private cars or public transportation tools, instead of replacing human drivers, e.g. bus, train, tram, ferry etc. Also in the future, machine-men can replace housewives to serve families to do housekeeping clean job , e.g. cleaning toilets, bathrooms, kitchens, even cooking functions at home. So (AI) machine-man can reduce housewives works at home. Moreover, (AI) machine man can take care old people , when who are living at homes or elder care centers.

So, it seems artificial intelligence (AI) will be possible developed to manufacture a new generation machine-man to assist (serve) families to do any simply cleaning or cooking jobs at homes. Moreover, the overall demand of (AI) general social needs will also rise, such as security, driving transportation tools, restaurant cleaning, elder centers care service etc. So, it seems that individual or families or social needs of (AI) will be increase in the future. Thus, it will influence macro economy growth (GDP) if there are large house family consumer group and hotel or bus or taxis or ferry etc. different business consumer group demand any artificial intelligence machine numbers increasing. Then, the artificial intelligence products and material manufacturers must need to buy many artificaial intelligence materials to produce any kinds of artificial intelligence machines to prepare to satisfy consumer individual needs. Consequently, macro economy will grow to the owned artificial intelligence development countries, e.g. US, China, UK.

● Why can artificial intelligence satisfy human needs on some service or manufacturing tasks to some occupations in our future societies?

First, On machine-man satisfactory demand aspect view point, it makes computers that think, it is the automation of activities. We associate with human thinking: like decision making, learning. It is the act of creating machine that perform function that require intelligence when performed by people. It is the study of mental faculties through the use of computational models. It is the study of computations that make it possible to perceive, reason and act. It is a branch of computer science that is concerned with the automation of intelligent behavior. It is anything in computing service that human don't yet know how to do property.

Second, on thought aspect artificial intelligence means systems thank think like humans, systems that think rationally.

Third, on behavioral aspect, artificial intelligence systems that act like human and that systems act rationally. However, the basic objective of (AI) is to represent human's thought processes in computation . These machines are supposed to exhibit behavior that. It is performed by a human being, would be considered intelligent. However, some authors feel (AI) has disadvantages, such as it is not creative, it is excited in the use of sensory devices, it can't make use of a very wide context of experiences and it does not use common sense.

For speech recognition and understanding function needs example, (AI) can be applied in speech recognition and understanding function, which (AI) speech or voice recognition is a data input method. For example, the computer recognizes and understands one (or a few) word commands. Speech understanding on the other hand is the computer's ability to understanding a spoken language. That is , the computer understands the meaning of sentences, an paragraphs through (AI).

So, (AI) can be attempted to learn human language how to speak. It is similar to translate human language skill, instead of actual human speaking skill. Also, (AI) can assist handicap learning or language student how to listen different languages by machine-man sounds from computers more accurately. So, it seems that it (AI) can replace human language teachers speaking function and can change teaching language nature of job in language speaking and listening education industry.

● Is artificial intelligence one good choice for human future technological raising productivities or improving performance advantages? Nowadays, new technology development is popular. However, artificial intelligence is one kind of new technology choice among different technologies innovation. So it brings this question: Is artificial intelligence technology value to invest? To answer this question. I shall indicate some other new technology developments to compare (AI) technology development to judge which has urgent needs to achieve human expectation nowadays.

For example, why is green peace interested in new technologies? New technologies features prominently in our ongoing campaigns against genetic modified crops and number power. However, which are also an integral part of our solutions to environmental challenges, including renewable energy technologies, such as solar, wind and wave (water) power energy as well as waste treatment technologies, such as mechanical, biological treatment.

It seems humans need concern how to apply (AI) technology to solve environment pollution challenges in our future. So, environment protective, agriculture, natural energy technology will be popular demand to attempt to apply (AI) technology to solve their challenges or apply (AI) to assist to develop their industry.

● How can artificial intelligence technology bring robotic invention needs more?

Advances in artificial intelligence (AI) technology and related fields have opened up new markets and new opportunities progress in critical areas, such as health, education, energy, economic development, social welfare and the environment pollution.

(AI) automation will continue to create wealth and expand the global economy development in the future. However, when many will benefits that growth won't be costless and will be accompanied by changes in the skills, that workers need to increase productivity in the economy and structural changes in the economy. So, in the skills that workers need to succeed in the economy and structural changes.

I shall indicate why aggressive policy action will be needed to help Americans who are disadvantaged by these changes , due to (AI) technology is caused. For automation industry change example, artificial intelligence (AI) capabilities will enable automation of some tasks that have long required human labor. These artificial intelligence technology introduction can increase new opportunities for individuals. The economy and society, but (AI) has also the potential to disrupt be current livelihoods of many Americans. However, (AI) leads to unemployment and increase in inequality over the long run depends not only on the (AI) technology itself, but also on the institutions and policies that are changed. Thus, it is possible that (AI) technology will raise some countries unemployment number if the employer apply (AI) technology workers to work instead of human labor in their factories, but it can also raise productivities for these employers.

Technological progress is main driver of growth of GDP per capita, allowing output to increase faster than labor and capital . However, technology can increase productivity, but also decrease the number of labor hours needed to create a unit of output. So (AI) causes unequal to labor wage decreases, even reduces the number of labor to manufacture, e.g. artificial intelligence technology of automation car manufacturing industry; clothing manufacturing industry; plane manufacturing etc. high technology of artificial intelligence manufacturing method. But (AI) should be potential environment benefit, although it raises unemployment ratio. Moreover, it can rise production , due to many skilled craft were replaced by the combination of machines and lower-skilled labor. The result of (AI) technology introduction , it causes output per hour risen when inequality declined, driving up average living standards, but the labor of some high-skill workers was no longer as valuable in the market. Otherwise, if (AI) technology is continue developed to be success. Some routine intensive occupations will be loss, which focused on predictable, e.g. easily programmable tasks, such as switchboard operators, filing clerks, travel agents, and assembly line workers would be particularly replaced by new (AI) technology. However, at the same time, (AI) technology development will bring these benefits: improvement in education (training (AI) technology scientists) , due to (AI) manufacturing technology needs are raising to businesses and institutional changes, such as the reduction in unionization and raising in the minimum wage to the (AI) manufacturing technology skilled labor in factories.

Because (AI) technology is not a single technology, but rather a collection of technologies that are applied to specific tasks, the effects of (AI) will be felt unevenly though the economy. It will bring some tasks will be most easily automated than others , and some jobs will be affected more than others, both negatively and positively. Finally, new jobs are likely to be directly created in areas , such as the development and supervision of (AI) as well as indirectly created in a range areas though out the economy as higher incomes lead to expanded demand.

However, if (AI) technology could dominate global labor markets. If labor productivity increases, do not influence into wage increases, then the large economic gains brought about by (AI) technology could be increased wealth inequality, due to employers can reduce production cost, but workers (labors) wages will not be increased, even will be decreased. Hence, it seems the (AI) technology will bring disadvantages to labor market to cause unemployment or reduce wages in possible, although it can reduce employer individual salary (wage) expenditure and it can raise productivity.

Artificial intelligence (AI) technology is a branch of computer science that aims to create intelligent machines that work and react like humans. So, (AI) is a technology that appears to impact (influence) human preference by learning, understanding complex contents, enhancing humans in executing both routine and non-routine tasks. In the future, (AI) technology that can be virtual personal assistant, as well as it may exist, such as robots with human-like processing capabilities.

How can (AI) technology impact global service and manufacturing industries products needs over the next 10 years? During this time period, (AI) technology is predicted to have wide-ranging applications including: Machine learning that automates analytical model building by using algorithms that allow machines to operate without human assistance.

In global education aspect, potential applications include predicting cause-and-effect relationships from biological data, identifying new drugs, self-driving cars, and protecting against fraud, improved natural language processing that allows computers to continue to better analysis, understand and generate language to interface with humans using natural human languages. For example, transcribing notes dictated by physicians, automatically drafting articles and translating text and speech. So (AI) technology can be applied to education aspect to improve humans' knowledge level.

In visual art aspect, (AI) machine vision that allows computers to identify objects, scenes and activities in images. Current applications of (AI) machine vision include providing objective descriptions for the blind seeing(visual) needs.

We except the economic effects of (AI) technology to include both direct GDP growth from sectors that develop or manufacture. (AI) technology and indirect GDP growth through increased productivity in existing sectors that employ some form of (AI). If (AI) technology is an increasingly critical component of more products, it will become an integral part of many people's lives. Thus, (AI)'s ability to influence economic activity, rather than the economic or development status of the region. (AI) has the potential to impact income classes and to bring significant gains to both developed and developing countries. For example, (AI) has the potential to optimize good production around the world by analyzing agricultural regions and identifying what is necessary to improve crop yields.

In estimating the future economic effects by (AI) technology innovation, it is important to note that it is challenging to accurately predict which applications of (AI) will ultimately be commercially successful. In micro level economic influence, we need to apply methodologies to estimate the economic effects of investment in firms developing (AI) technology since investment levels in a technology are a telling sign of the future potential of that (AI) technology.

How (AI)'s development may affect the global economy over the next ten years. In fact, (AI) technology has the potential to affect business across the global in a wide range of industries in ways only a number of technologies have done in the parts. For example, (AI) technology's expected to be a useful tool for enhancing human capabilities and in some instances replacing functions, such as driving a car, adoption of broadband internet, mobile telephone, industrial robotic automation have served to enhance human capabilities.

However, significant public debate has focused on projections of (AI) technology's effect on the labor force. However, large companies prefer to invest in (AI) technological industry. For example, face book's (AI) research lab., google machine intelligence lab. and micro soft machine learning and artificial intelligence research division are all making advances in (AI) technology and investing in the industry's top talent. Additionally, between 2010 year and 2015 year, nearly $5 billion in venture capital funding invested in firms across the global developing and employing (AI) technology (Facebook (AI) Research).

● How can artificial intelligence impact on workplace on future service or manufacturing industries ?

Modern information technologies and the labor economy growth of machines is powered by artificial intelligence have already strongly influenced the world of work in the 21 ST century. Computers, algorithms and software simplify every tasks and it is impossible to image how most of our life could be managed without them. How can be the information economy characterized by exponential growth replaces the most production industry based on economy of scales? What will the future world of work look like and how long will it take to get? Will the future world of work be a world where humans spend less time earning their livelihood? Alternatively, are mass unemployment, mass poverty and social distortions also possible scenario for the future, where robots, artificial intelligence systems play an increasingly central role? These questions concern how artificial intelligence further development . Can influence labor economy growth on workplace ? When the labor market has widespread impact on intelligence property, information technology, product liability, competition and labor and employment laws.

How (AI) technology impacts on labor workplace.

The future influence any organizations how labor economies use of (AI) can be analyzed, such as deep machine learning is based on a set of model high level data. Unlike human workers, the machines are connected the whole time in workplace. If one machine makes a mistake, all autonomous systems will keep this in mind and will avoid the same mistake the next time.

Over the long run intelligent machines will win against every human expert. Production robots have been replacing employees because of the (AI) technology. They work more precisely than humans and cost loss. Creative solutions like 3D printers and the self learning ability of these production robots will replace human workers, the automatic data recording and data processing, traditional back office activities are no longer in demand. Autonomous software will collect necessary information and will send it to the employee who needs it. Additionally, dematerialization leads to the phenomenon that traditional physical products are becoming software. For example, CD or DVDs are being replaced by streaming services. The replacement of traditional event ticket, e-travel ticket service products or hard cash will be the next step, due to the possibility of payment by smartphone. So, (AI) technology will impact human's daily life consumption behaviors in the future. For another example, transportation tools, such as boats and ferries and private vehicles will use sensors and navigating without human input. Taxi and truck drivers will become obsolete, the stock store applies to stock managers and postal carriers of the delivery is distributed by (AI) machine delivery method.

● Can (AI) technology impact on customer relationship management (CRM) on customer service tasks market ?

Nowadays , (AI) is a technology almost as old as the computer industry itself, it is similar with the advent of personal assistants function to businesses and personal promotion channel, such as (Amazon's Alexa, Apple's Siri, Google's Assistant) image recognition (face book), personalized recommendations (Netflix , Amazon). Those innovations have been driven by a increase in processing power, lower cost hardware, and the exploding creation and availability of data. It seems, (AI) technology can impact global customer service management method.

How to forecast economic impact modeling to (AI) will affect global economy? Can human forecast business revenue growth and job creation (or destruction) based on (AI) applied to customer relationship management (CRM) activities? In addition to the economic impact on (AI) or (CRM) which can include an estimate of the economic impact attributable to sales forces customer base. What can economic benefits be brought to (CRM) from (AI) technology?

Artificial intelligence(AI) comprises a set of technologies that use natural language processing, machine learning, knowledge graphs, and other tools to answer questions, discover insights and provide recommendations. Computer systems can use (AI) hypothesize and formulate possible answers based on available evidence can be trained through the ingestion of vast amounts of content, and automatically adapt and learn from (AI) self mistakes and failures.

So, any business organizations (customer service departments) can provide efficient and effective customer relationship management of excellent customer service quality if which applied (AI) technology system. The different type of (AI) systems include: (AI) system platforms, machine learning (AI) based data preparation and enrichment tools, machine vision/ image recognition, voice speech recognition, text analysis and natural language processing, bots , e.g. face book website and virtual digital assistance solutions, social media pattern analysis , sentiment analysis, advanced numerical analysis (e.g. IOT streaming , machine logs), supporting technologies, knowledge base dialog management, Q&A processing etc. different (AI) technology system customer relationship management (CRM) tools.

(AI) (CRM) of activity can include these categories, such as: corporate marketing, marketing operation, field marketing, customer support, digital commerce, customer analytics, customer influenced product or service design, product or service pricing, finance information, presentation, customer billing, inventory , logistics and fulfilment support, partner management etc. different CRM tools.

(AI) technology of CRM has been carrying on plan different stages to achieve CRM personal assistant tool for businesses. The stages are such as, in the beginning stage of (AI) projects in place, implement now, pilot phase next year in the final stage of (AI) customer relationship management tools are foreseeable future. So, this CRM technology has been improved to plan in different stages every year to prepare to achieve full capacity of CRM service quality for businesses to use in the future.

Hence, how to develop an estimate prediction of the economic impact (AI) technologies could have CRM activities, which depends on gathering macroeconomic information on business revenue and the basic marketing of business revenue and the basic markup of business expenses by major functions (customer support, marketing and sales , production etc.)

An economic impact model that can gather data together and forecast the results how (AI) artificial intelligence technology brings (CRM) customer relationship management benefits to businesses, e.g. surveys investigation includes IT spending by sample countries, GDP and population estimates and forecasts, revenue per employee and ratios of IT spend to GDP. Surveys (questionnaire questions) of forecast results are influenced by (AI) impact can include: results are projected from surveys and rely on estimates are made by respondents on the expected financial improvements in categories of (AI) –assisted customer relationship management activities. The forecast assumes that these estimates are correct; financial estimates are based on estimates of "first year" improvement from full (AI) implementation; forecasts are from planning to implement any artificial intelligence of customer relationship management (CRM) projects, the improvement forecast is of categories of activity , e.g. corporate marketing , digital commerce, and customer analytics. They are not estimates of ROI for the (AI) software. They rely on conservative estimates to which each of these entities might affect company revenue, expenses or productivity. They also rely on estimates of the penetration of software in customer relationship management activities . Net new jobs created are based on the ratio of new revenue to jobs required to support that revenue . They can assume that 50% of the net new revenue will support increases in labor and the rest will go for capital and other operating expenses that may replace jobs lost to automation.

In the future, some of the ways in micro economic benefits to any organizations. (AI) technology is expected to impact CRM activities include: Spending up sales cycles, improving lead generation and qualification solving customer support problems faster (raising service quality), helping companies improve brand campaigns and recognition, lowering costs of support calls when increasing resolution rates, lowering the cost of recruiting employees and partners, increasing revenue from optimized product marketing, optimizing price, distribution logistics and preventing loss through fraud detection. So, micro economic benefits view point, it seems that (AI) CRM technology can raise any companies economic benefits for care term.

Artificial intelligence enables machines or the in-build software to behave like human beings which allows these decisions and act. The advent of (AI) is leading , talking, making decisions and act. The advent of (AI) is leading to new technologies advances and transforming the economic and employment opportunities for humans in a positive way. (AI) related technologies can facilitate our live. For example, industrial robotics, robotic medical assistants, smart games, financial forecasting software, big data analysis, algorithms in health and bioinformatics, pilotless cargo places, drone ambulances and general purpose and workplace robots and others. (Disruptors technologies: Advances that will transform life, business and the global economy).

Artificial intelligence also known as computational intelligence is defined as " the human –like intelligence exhibited by machines or software. It is theorized that intelligence of humans can be described and intelligence machines or software can simulate it. These machines software can be reasonable , learn, perceive and process information, like human mind and thus facilitate human life. They can think and act for us. So, artificial intelligence is an interdisciplinary field of study including computer science, neuroscience, psychology, linguistics and philosophy.

However, (AI) research and developments have economically impacted many industries, such as robotics, telecommunications, computer applications , health, finance, heavy manufacturing, transportation, aviation, e-service and e-commerce, military , music and movie, toys and games entertainment etc. industries.

In fact, many ideas, systems and technologies have been developing in the world of (AI) technology. However, which are net called or considered (AI) products, rather which are mentioned with their specific names, such as smart graphics, machine learning, e-commerce etc. (i.e. this is called (AI) effect).

● How can (AI) technology influence digital industry ?

Nowadays, (AI) related industrial applications will replace most human power in fields, including call centers, customer services and air cargo transportation. (AI) technologies also help weather forecasting based on repeated rainfall pattern (data) recognition, through robotics (i.e. floor cleaning, moving lawns etc.) transporting people and products with unmanned vehicles, sending space unmanned smart shuttles, developing robotic arms, predicting market values in stock exchanges by internet, making homes safer, helping elderly and disabled using robotic servants etc.

Among the (AI) related technologies , there are a few that significance for the impact on society and especially on digital economy . (AI) is particularly influential in machine learning. Such as robotics, transportation, finance, health and bioinformatics, e-commerce , e-games, big online data gathering and internet-of-things. For example, machine e-learning is based in bioinformatics and robots that can learn new skills for better caregiving in healthcare. What is machine e-learning? Machines can e-learn from e-data gathering, coming up generalizations and making decisions to act in certain ways from internet.

There are important applications , such as e-machine perception, electronic online natural language learning processing, online search engines, online bioinformatics, online brain –computer interface, online game playing, online robot locomotion, online advertising, online computations finances, online health monitoring, online DNA classification and decision making, online in chemistry –cheminformatics . So, online machine learning can positively impact productivity and it can enhance information and analytical system from (AI) online channel.

What is robotics? Robotics is one of the most strongly influenced fields in (AI). For example, heavy manufacturing industries, robots and used and man power is replaced for effectiveness, precision, and accuracy, especially in respective or dangerous tasks, including welding, assembling , picking and placing .

So, robots can acquire new skills or adapt the changing dynamic environment. Also, artificial intelligence can be applied in developing transportation. For example, automated vehicles, driver assistance systems

, safety systems, collision avoidance systems and public transportation. Moreover, (AI) technology has proven to produce some of the best tools to predict stock market fluctuations from internet data gathering method. It's predictions are based on ever-evolving predictions algorithms and systems learn new models and make connections between historical data and new data to measure stock market trading more accurate from internet data gathering channel.

In health field, especially in health data processing , analysis, decision making support and medical diagnosis. So, online data can show which patients will need what treatment and what alternative drugs could be used more accurate from (AI) online data gathering method. Bioinformatics is an interdisciplinary field combining statistics, (AI) online technology can help in discovering data patterns and modeling through the application of machine learning, artificial neural networks and genetic algorithms. For example, further (AI) technology development of human genome project of online data sequences.

Online shopping can be facilitated by virtual assistants developed through (AI) technology and these assistants can offer the best advice. (AI) online purchase coming after every product image recommendations and personalization bring important revenue to shopping online sites, like Amazon . Smart computer graphics and games, artificial intelligence is useful in smarter computer, graphics, scene modeling , scene rendering processes in order to create, for example, effective human –robot interactions , online machine learning, online strategic games techniques etc. online computer related (AI) software.

So, online big data analysis and big data does have a critical need in the world of online intelligence machines and software in our future. In other words, (AI) offers online technology to enable online big data analysis to provide industrial organizations with valuable information for effective decision making in short time. For example, what IBM's Watson achieved: this machine used 200 million of structured and unstructured content with a special technology of hypothesis generation, massive evidence gathering, analysis and scoring from internet channel.

Finally, (AI) online technology another related internet invention (internet of things) (IOT) is the network of machines or objects connected through internet. These connected objects can sense their internal and external environment, communicate with each other, can send critical data and finally can make decisions to act or correct their environment from (AI) online technology. For example, factories can monitor and automatically change production processes, hospitals can monitor and regulate the health conditions of their patients , schools can collect data from facilities and cars can send data to car makers from (AI) online technology.

Partner predicts that (IOT) market will create about trillion amount value by 2020 year. Although machines collect big data from their environment, whether which gain an insight or learn from these online data largely depends on the (AI) online machine learning principals and (AI) online technology. In 2013, Mckinsey estimated that disruptive technologies closely related with potential economic impact in 2025 year between \$7.1 to \$13.1 trillion amount (automation of knowledge work, advanced robotics, autonomous or near-autonomous vehicles).

● Could work activities in China be automated

making on service or manufacturing industries needs in the nation with the world's largest automation potential?

Can (AI) technology influence China economy? Could China workers be affected and jobs made up of routine work activities and predictable? Will programmable tasks be particularly impact to China employment market ? When impact on labor market is likely to be gradual at the aggregate level, it can be sudden and dramatic at the level of specific work activities, rending some job obsolete fairly. Overall (AI) technology will raise digital skills when reducing demand for medium incomer inequality for China workers. It seems (AI) technology's effect on productivity could be crucial to China's future economic growth as the population ages are increasing.

In China, some biggest technological companies driving significant investments in research and development. Moreover, China is one of the leading global (AI) technology development county. However, China will need to focus on building its innovation capacity. For example, United States and United Kingdom are currently producing more influential (AI) technological research. However, if China planed to achieve (AI) technology success, it's traditional industries will need to develop technical know-how –to and overcoming implementation costs prepare to develop (AI) . When (AI) technology is introduced into China society, China government needs to raise concerning ethical, legal, technological security etc. business questions. Also, surrounding issues include privacy, discrimination, legal liability and regulation. It aims to encourage overseas investors to choose to invest (AI) technological industry to raise GDP growth and manufacturing industries income growth for long term in China.

If China encouraged overseas (AI) technology investment in its country. It is possible to influence China employment market to be changed. Because (AI) technology will impact to influence China people daily life. Due to (AI) technology is introduced to China society, many rich people will prefer to spend to buy any high (AI) technological products for entertainment or learning or machine man driving etc. daily necessity activities. Then it will raise GDP growth and will raise (AI) manufacturers or related-(AI) technological manufacturers profit. It is beneficial to China because it can become one high knowledgeable and (AI) technological economical society. But it will bring bad influences to raise unemployment chance for the low skillful labor. In labor economy aspect influence , how (AI) technology can influence China low skillful labor unemployment ratio raising. The raising low skill labor unemployment reason is because China low skillful human labors are argued or are replaced by (AI) technology creating new challenges to introduce to influence China society of simply human manufacturing job nature to be changed to be high (AI) technology manufacturing job nature in any China factories. Moreover, when (AI) technology introduction to China, it will cause other related social challenges in China. The varied (AI) related challenges, including the difficulty of creating safe and reliable hardware for sensing and affecting (transportation and education), the challenges of gaining public trust, a low resource comities and public safety and security, the challenges of overcoming fears or marginalizing humans in China employment and workplace and the risk of diminishing interpersonal trust because the low skillful labors won't believe any China employers will give chance to employ them , due to (AI) technology will replace their skills and man manufacturing of productivity is much less to compare to (AI) technology manufacturing method.

● How does (AI) technology influence the future of employment change?

Are future nature of jobs changed to computerization from (AI) technology? Where are the probability of computing occupations from (AI) technology influence? What is expected impacts of future computing on labor market from (AI) technology influence? John Maynard Keynes's frequently cited prediction of widespread technological unemployment " du to our discovery of means of economic the use of labor outrunning the pace of which we can find new used of labor" (Keynes, 1933, p.3).

In the future, (AI) technology will impact some nature of occupations to change computing. This chance will also influence some countries' economic change. For example, some factory human labors hand routine manufacturing tasks will be changed to computerization of routine manufacturing tasks by (AI) technological machine men hand manufacturing method. it will cause a structured shift in the labor market, with workers reallocating their labor supply from middle-income manufacturing to low-income service occupations.

Arguably, this is because the manual tasks of service occupations are less computerization, as who require a higher degree of flexibility and physical adaptability. So, (AI) technology will influence the human hand labor skillful occupation nature of task cheaper , such as vehicle manufacturing , ship manufacturing, computer manufacturing, steel manufacturing, television, radio etc. home electronic products of heavy machine industry change. Due to (AI) technology machine man will be proper to be used to manufacturing these electronic products when the (AI) technology innovation can develop to the mature stage. Then, any countries manufacturers will choose to use (AI) technology machine man, instead of human hand production.

Supposing the future prices of computing are fallen, seriously, problem solving skills are becoming relatively productive, explaining the substantial employment growth in manufacturing occupations, involving cognitive tasks where skilled labor has a comparative advantage, as well as the increase education needs for (AI) technology computing of machine man subject study.

Prediction of education needs for (AI) technology student numbers will increase, due to manufacturing industry needs many (AI) technology students in future employment market. Another (AI) technology influence if the future (AI) technological innovation, e.g. machine man manufacturing or machine man service industries will both increase demand, then with more sophistic software technologies will be disrupted labor markets by marketing workers redundant.

For publishing industry, what is striking about the case in paper book publishing industry will be unpopular? Due to the electronic book publishing industry will be popular, e.g. Amazon publish . (AI) technology can influence paper book manufacturing method which is replaced by machine man electronic book manufacturing method as well as it will cause the computerization is no longer confined to routine manufacturing tasks. Due to (AI) machine man manufacturing technology will be proper to be used to manufacture any products in short time efficiently and effectively , e.g. electronic book products. In the future, if it is fact to occur this case, such as (AI) technological machine man manufacturing method will be adopted (applied) to manufacture electronic books or any products in possible. (AI) technology will cause many manufacturing workers are unemployed. It is beneficial to employers, who can reduce to spend much wages expenditure to employ manufacturing workers, but it will cause many manufacturing workers loss jobs and reduce income to support whose families lives. It will cause social challenges, e.g. increasing stealing crimes if the manufacturing workers had not other skills to find other jobs to do easily. So, manufacturers need to concern over technological unemployment which will be hardly future phenomenon if who decided to dismiss all manufacturing workers, due to (AI) technology machine men replace to them.

If (AI) technology can be innovated to produce any kinds of machine man to serve any service or manufacturing industries successfully. Then, it will bring these questions: Can future that workers be influenced to be automation employment and productivity by (AI) technology influence? Does it impact to influence the (AI) technology countries' productivity and growth and natural resources development and labor markets and evolution of global financial markets and economic impact of technology and innovation and urbanization etc. issues? How will automation transform the workplace? What will be the implication for employment? What is likely to be its impact both on productivity in the global economy and on employment?

In fact, automatic of activities can enable businesses to improve performance by reducing errors chance and improving quality and speed, and same cases achieving outcomes that go beyond human capabilities. Some economists indicate (AI) technology would give a needed boost to economic growth and prosperity have of the working age population in many countries. Based on the scenario modeling, they estimate automation could raise productivity growth globally by 0.8 to 1.4 % annually. They also indicated that almost half the activities people are almost $1.6 trillion in wages to do in the global economy have the potential to be automated adapting current demonstrates technology, according to their analysis of more than 2,000 work activities across 800 occupations. When less than 5% of all occupations can be automated entirely using demonstrated technology, about 60% of all occupations have at least 30% of worker made activities, that would be automated. More occupation will change to be automated. They also indicated for business performance benefits of automation are relatively clear, but the issues are more complicated by policy making to attract foreign investors. Beyond technical feasibility, the cost of technology, competition labor will include skills and supply and demand dynamics, performance benefits and beyond labor cost savings and social and regulatory acceptance will affect the automation. Their predictions suggest that half of today work activities could be automated by 2055 year, but this could happen 10 to 20 years earlier or latter depending on the various factors in addition to their wider economic condition.

Some scientists suggest (AI) technology is finally starting to deliver real-life business benefits. Computer power is growing significantly , algorithms are becoming more sophisticated and perhaps most important of all, the world is generating vast quantities of the fuel that powers (AI) technology data billions of gigabytes of it every day. Also, online firms are digital natives, such as Google online search service company is investing on (AI) technology. For new though most of the news if coming from the suppliers of (AI) technologies. And many new users are only in the experimental phase. Few products are on the market or are likely to arrive these soon to drive immediate and widespread adoption. As a result, analysts believe (AI) technology's potential will give true economic benefit in the future. (AI) industry will introduce to suppliers and users to raise economic potential of (AI) technology.

In the future, (AI) technology systems can solve business problems. Some scientists categorized those into five technology systems that are key areas of (AI) technology development: robotics and autonomous vehicles, computer vision language virtual agents and machine learning , which is based on algorithms that learn from data without replying on rules-based programming in order to draw conclusions or direct an action.

Such as computer vision and language includes natural language processing, analytics, speech recognition technology, some are about learning from information, such as about machine learning and others are related to acting on information, such as robotics, autonomous vehicles and virtual agents, which are computer programs that can converse with humans. Machine learning and a subfield called deep learning are artificial intelligence applications.

Artificial intelligence (AI) is a term first defined in 1956 year. It is a branch of computer science that aims to create intelligent machines that work and react like humans. In contrast today, 60 years later, (AI) is characterized by a number of applications, including computers playing games against humans and understanding human languages, virtual personal assistants, and robotics which involve computers seeing , hearing and reacting to sensory stimuli. In the future, technologists predict for (AI) technology ranging from (AI) being used as a tool to aid relatively simple processes for robots with human like mental capabilities, who expect (AI) technology can emulate human performance by learning, coming to mind its own conclusions, understanding complex content, engaging in dialog with people, enhancing human cognitive performance or replacing humans in executing both routine and non-routine tasks. In existing industry, (AI) technology is used , such as targeted advertising and virtual used personal assistant as well as the (AI) technology that my exist in the future, such as robots with human vehicle processing capabilities.

The range of (AI) technology's progress in the future will determine the economic impact future of (AI) technology on the global economy with more limited advances and applications (i.e. weak (AI) only) corresponding to more limited economic impacts and more substantial progress, i.e. strong (AI) technology is corresponding to more significant economic impact.

(AI) technology learning that automates analytical model, including predicting cause-and-effect relationship from biological data, identifying new drugs, self-driving cars and protecting against fraud etc. functions. Also (AI) learning can improve natural language processing that allows computers to continue to better analyze, understand and generate language to interface with human using the natural human language, virtual personal assistant, helps users by providing scheduling appointment, reminds organizing personal finance and finding providers of various services, machine vision allows (AI) machine man to identify object, scenes and activities in detect pedestrians and bicyclists.

We expect the economic effects of (AI) technology to include both direct GDP growth from sectors that develop or manufacture (AI) technology and indirect GDP growth through increased productivity in existing sectors that employ some from of (AI) technology. If (AI) producing sectors could grow, then it could lead to increase revenues and employment of (AI) technological professionals within these existing firms as well as the potential creation of entirely new economic activities to any countries' societies productivity improvement in existing sectors could be realized through faster and move efficient processes and decision making as well as increased (AI) technological knowledge and access to information available in societies easily.

In the future, if (AI) technology is an increasingly critical component of more products, it will become an integral part of necessary products of many people's lives. The extent of (AI)'s economy effort is also likely to vary from region to region, thought variation may be more dependent on the predominate economic activity of a region and the (AI) ability can influence economic activity, rather then the economic or developmental status of the regions. (AI) technology can move accessibility and can use source development to do international business between one country and another country.

So (AI) technology has the potential to give benefits to different income chooses and to bring significant gains to both developed and developing countries. For agricultural technology, (AI) has the potential to optimize food production around the world by analyzing agricultural regions and identifying what is necessary to improve crop yield. In total, (AI) technology gives greater economic impact to any countries agricultural regions if which implemented (AI) technology to grow crop , fruit etc. food production in the farms.

Investment in (AI) technology is such as capital investment to any countries' public or private enterprises. So, it will have large economic impact to the future . If the (AI) technology is reasonable invested to the different needs aspect by the public or private enterprises in the country. Then, it will have good economic impact to the country in the future. However, when (AI) technology is likely to affect both the productivity and employment components of economic growth in many sectors. Significant public debate has focused on projections of (AI)'s effect on the labor force. However, for instance, some researchers have argued that the rise of (AI) technology and automation will led to significant unemployment as capital is substituted for the low skillful labor. So, they point to the concern that the increasing sophistication of (AI) technology may balance skilled and semi-skilled workers and the reduce the size of the middle class. However, this is not a new argument, due to (AI) technology negatively affecting the labor force and leading to mass unemployment. Because the (AI) technology is the substitution of machinery for human labor. Although, employment in certain industries, has been reduced in the past due to technological advancement. For long term, the labor market has adapted to the introduction of new technology, giving rise to new jobs in new areas. (AI) technology may also be accomplished without a reduction to total employment in the long-term to some Asia countries, such as Hong Kong and Japan. Because Hong Kong and Japan many low skilled labor, e.g. security, cleaner who complaint that employers need them to work long time hours. (abnormal working hours) e.g. one day 12 to 15 working hour per day. Hence, if (AI) machine means invention technology success. Security or cleaning job can be worked from (AI) machine man in some hours every day in order to reduce the long time working hours cleaners or security workers, e.g. one (AI) machine man works 4 hours for cleaning or security job, one day as well as another cleaner or security labor only needs to work 8 hours one day. So total security or cleaning employers can employ 12 hours machine cleaners or security workers and human cleaners or security workers in one day. For long term benefit, Hong Kong or Japan every security or cleaning worker does not need to work 12 hours minimum working hours one day. They won't feel tried and bore and without private with whose families, so who will accept to do these cleaning or security jobs, even they can raise work efficient and performance when who feel happy and health.

So, (AI) technology of machine man invention can raise low skillful labor efficiency and it can help them to avoid abnormal working hours demand in some busy work life countries, such as Hong Kong and Japan. Before, one Japan female labor feel unhappy to work, due to who often needs to work abnormal working hours for her employer and who has less sleeping and without any private time to enjoy her life with her families every day. So this abnormal working hours factor causes her to do commit suicide behavior, then she is die unlucky. So (AI) technology of machine man invention ought avoid abnormal working hours demand for employer in any countries in the future.

The most important occurrence to any employers, some researchers had attempted to do one experiment to find that private research and development , venture capital and public research and development investment all have strong net effect or economic growth with venture capital funding further having the strongest such effect from (AI) technology. The researchers hypothesize the venture capital investment contributes to economic growth through (AI) technology innovation and by the capacity of an economy to use existing (AI) technology knowledge to increase productivity. They predict the impacts of venture capital, business-research and development and public research and development can raise multi factor productivity from (AI) technology introduction.

Can (AI) technology influence the economic development to developing countries? The developing regions of the world contain most of natural resources. If one day, (AI) technology has invent one kind of machine man which can assist any gas or oil workers to seek any new oil/gas natural resource locations easily. I believe that (AI) technology can help these natural resource exploitation countries will gain economic benefit more easily. So, (AI) driven technology can be used to change to create any new opportunities to address poor management or resources and improve human well being, such as Africa Latin America and India can use (AI) technology machine man to seek any oil/gas natural resource countries exploitation activities to attempt to gain much economic benefits.

● Why will (AI) technology influence future service and manufacturing workers needs ?

Nowadays, increases in capital and labor are no longer driving the levels of economic growth, such as (AI) technology. The ability of increase in capital investment and in labor of traditional drivers of production, have no longer to be enjoyed in most developed economies ,e.g. developed country, US, UK . However, artificial intelligence has the potential to overcome the physical limitation of capital and labor to avoid missing out on this opportunity. So, policy makers and business leaders must prepare for and work toward a future with artificial intelligence. They must do with the idea that (AI) is another simply method to enhance productivity method . Rather they must see (AI) as the tool that can transform thinking about how growth is created.

Economists have always thought of new technologies are as driving growth their ability to enhancing. It can replace labor and capital factor of production. So, it brings this question: What is the factor of production (AI) technology characteristics. They key factor is to see (AI) technology as a capital-labor .

(AI) can replicate labor activities at much greater scale and speed, and to even perform some tasks began the capabilities of human. For example, by using virtual assistants , 1000 legal documents can be reviewed in a matter of days instead of taking three people six moths to complete. Some (AI) technology may be one kind of factor of production in the future. For another example, people will work in workplace digitalization environment. So, in the future, working environment and information management are automated. Such as Konica camera sale company will use workplace digitalization. So , (AI) technology can provide workplace digitalization in order to raise productivity efficiency. (AI) technology will be one kind of production which is replaced by workplace digitalization and it will grow any organization productivity efficiently. Then, (AI) technology will assist overall social economy growth , due to productivity is raised and products can be produced in short time to prepare to sell in consumption market. So, time will be shortened to increase GDP growth fast for the development of (AI) technology countries.

What will be the development of (AI) technology and predictions concerning the future evolution? The computers and robots will develop conscious, intelligent and minds into humans, enhancing psychological and behavioral abilities and allowing for direct communication with (AI) minds. (AI) technology will be impacted human life by (AI) technology information communicative and environmental influence. A " world brain" and " world mind", this psychological system will be enhanced and enriched the capacities of both individual and collective cognition by (AI) technology of service industries.
(AI) technology with influence these human needs of service industries changes, such as , biological science, finance, entertainment, business, biological science, transportation, communication military etc. The personal computer evolution, the internet and the world wide web which exploded on the scene, linking business, homes, schools, social organizations which were a completely unpredicted phenomenon to influence human life. Kurzweil (1999) predicts that by 2029 year, most human communication will be with machines. According to Person, by 2100 year, there will be human machine convergence.
How can (AI) technology influence environmental protection to make benefits to farming economic growth? (AI) technology can be applied to predict how to solve environmental pollution challenge to avoid to damage any crop or vegetable or rice or fruit etc. food growth. Because environmental experts can gather global environmental pollution data from an environmental database to build a perform a systematic analysis from (AI) technology. The first step is this broad analysis can include understanding, statistical and data gathering techniques to obtain the relevant data, the correlation among the variables involved, and a list of possible models. The next step is to select a set of methods and models that

cover all kinds of knowledge and functionalities needed for the decision making process. Once the models are selected, they must be fully implemented by means of machine learning , data mining, statistical or numerical technique. After that, those models must be integrated to build the whole EDSS. The EDSS must be tested to check its performance, accuracy, usefulness and reliability, both from the user's and (AI) technology/computer scientist's point of view. If these is any wrong feature in any development stage, such as model's integration, models' implementation, selection of models, database, problem analysis etc. the developers must come back in the update th required components. When the evaluation phase is all right, the EDSS is ready to be applied to the environment. The great contribution of artificial intelligence to EDSS the integration of several methods complementing the classical statistical models/simulation , statistical analysis, linear models, etc. and numerical models (control algorithms, optimization techniques etc.) .

This cooperation makes the resulting systems more reliable and powerful in coping with real world environment systems. Date interpretation has been a principal area of research in (AI) technology since the very beginning. The most demanding problem in the environmental assessment context. Knowledge representation permits the definition of the different types of data that the existing methods adapt to the process. There is also a lot of work to clean, repair and transform the huge available quantities of raw data. Apart from this, the availability of meta-information or background knowledge is required to guide the process. Data mining is multi-disciplinary: It covers expert systems, data based technology, statistics, data visualization and unsupervised machine learning. These techniques operate at the level of data and background information, where numerous and often incompatible new commensurate pieces of information from disparate sources have to be brought together (K, Fedra, 1994).

So, it seems that in the future, (AI) technology with the increasing maturity in particular those related to knowledge and engineering, new dimensions can be assisted to users in environmental decision making are available. For example, many environmental systems are characterized both by incomplete models and by limited data. Hence, in the future, (AI) technology will be applied to predict climate change to reduce crop or fruit etc. food agriculture challenge by climate change bad influence.

● Will (AI) technology influence taxi transport service needs ?

To understand how the manufacturing business must adapt to prosper in the technology, we need to understand how (AI) technology will change us to shape our daily habits to satisfy our expectation of products to how we shop and even the immediate of the entire process. For example, taxi services are in the crosshairs as on demand transportation services like, available of the touch of a smart phone button expand. In fact, Yellow lab, US country , san Francisco city's largest taxi company is filing for bankruptcy as the industry starts to change faster than almost anyone expected. However, at this point, its more than an app that is changing, some our taxi passengers renting taxi transportation to catch consumption behavior.

(AI) technology will influence digital economy for taxi passenger's individual customer experience, offering a growing renting taxi to catch of service and feedback opportunities when any one taxi passenger who chooses to use mobile phone app online tool to prepaid to rent any taxi more easily.

Also in the long term, (AI) technology can influence vehicles drive themselves of behavior. Already, companies like Google and GM are working on projects to bring fleets of autonomous vehicles to cities at the path of a button.

Moreover, this on-demand service model is beginning to appear across a much broader range of markets. For example , Amazon company is investing in its own fleet of trucks, planes and even drone at the same time as it pushes for same-day delivery of products. As some point, vehicles will be autonomous too. So, it seems that (AI) technique will influence any transportations choose to use digital autonomous driving technology in the future . For Amazon company case, it is not stopping of logistics. It is also aiming to automatically manage the supply of consumer home products with its recently launched Amazon replenishment service, Dash. Dash is a digital service that enables that connected derive to automatically order physical products from Amazon when supplies are running low. So, it seems (AI) technology will be applied to logistic function by digital technology method introduction in the future.

Hence autonomous vehicles will optimize industry supply chains and logistics operations through increased efficiency and flexibility. In fact, fully automated and lean supply chains will keep reduce load sizes and inventory by leveraging smart distribution technologies and smaller autonomous vehicles by machine man assistance. If Amazon continues to grow market share for online sales by reducing effort required by the consumer to place an order, when also contributing the almost immediate delivery of products to the doorstep. So, it will further fuel the trend toward on-demand derive. As Amazon company fuels the on-demand economy, consumers will expect immediacy in more parts of the digital economy. On top of speed, consumers increasing expect more personalization options.

So, (AI) technology will influence digital manufacturing, such as Amazon publishing to monitor every aspect of every process in real -time and communicating to self-optimized deep learning robotics, new methods of high volume and high customization will become possible. Then, as products merge into product platforms and even services, manufacturers have the opportunity to provide components and platforms used by smaller players. So, (AI) technology will influence manufacturing industry to choose automated SMI lines, robots installed, automation engineers.

Another future (AI) technology development can be applied to space science aspect, such as Automation engineering space in manufacturing process to achieve digital manufacturing benefits to any businesses in the future. Such as reducing cost, shortening manufacturing time, raising efficiency, shortening delivery products to client individual time. How can artificial intelligence give the need and advanced fast and evaluation methods benefits for space exploration? When US NASA (space exploration organization) achieves any space exploration missions, it will answer this question:

When is it useful to have a machine use (AI) technology to achieve a decision? After all, after millions of years of space exploration and rough 10,000 years of civilization, humans are usually quite good at making decisions in complex uncertain environments. Through, Johns Hoplains University's Applied Physical Lab. Research in (AI) technology enabled systems, which has identified three general use cases for (AI) technology to explore space mission:

First, for some tasks (AI) technology is more cost effectiveness than human. Second, (AI) technology is better suited than humans at solving some, but not all problems. Third, (AI) technology allows NASA organization's space exploration mission to develop machines that ate capable of responding faster than when a human is in the decision loop (D. Scheidt, 2012, A. Castano et. al. 2008).

So, the use of (AI) technology to enable science by observing the pace of rapidly evolving phenomena was demonstrated. It is more effectively coordinating and (AI) technology utilizing to earn economic benefits to use for space exploration mission.

However, (AI) technology also have current risk for space exploration. Today (AI) technology is immature and requires further development to reach its potential. For instance, the (AI) technology algorithms that detected the dust derive could not have identified whether the Martain weather represented a threat to the cover. Also it can not yet use instrument input to determine what, where and how to autonomously make the next space science measurement. An equally important factor limiting (AI)'s deployment is that lacks the methodology and technology to effectively test (AI) technology. So, the challenge will testing (AI) enabled system is how (AI) performance can be measured. It would be NASA organization's difficulty to find (AI) technology to develop to carry on researching any space exploration missions in the future. However, (AI) technology will be a good economic benefit choice for space exploration mission in the future.

● What is artificial intelligence potential benefits and ethical considerations to influence future global job market change?

The ability of (AI) technology systems to transform vast amounts of complex information into insight has the potential to help solve manufacturing or service challenges for human needs. However, to reap the societal benefits of (AI) systems, humans will need to trust then and make sure that which follow the same ethical principles, moral values, professional codes and social norms that we humans would follow in the same scenario, research and educational efforts as well as carefully designed regulation in order to achieve the most effort of economic benefits goals. For example, international business machines corporation (IBM) is actively engaged both competitors , in global discussions about how to make (AI) ethical and as beneficial as possible for people as social economic benefits.

(AI) is usually defined as the " capability of a computer program to perform tasks or reasoning processes " that human usually associate to intelligence in a human being. Often, it has to do with the ability to make a good decision, even when there is uncertainty, too much information to handle. As an example, play chess or complex card games of entertainment activities is believed to need some form of intelligence in a human being, as well as choosing the best medical facilities in a difficult medical case, or creating something new, such as mathematical theorem or even some form of act, or even driving automatic machine man (self driving vehicle) replacing human driving in the middle of a crowded city.

(AI) needs depends on what we consider being intelligence in the behavior of a human being act a certain point in time. If human belief about human intelligence changes and we don't believe any longer that a certain task requires intelligence, then a computer program performing that task is no longer part of (AI), it becomes just another boring computer program. So, it means that (AI) technology will replace some old computer programs, if human can invent new generation of (AI) software for any functions or activities to satisfy human needs.

As IBM, it argues intelligence. This means that we aim to build systems that enhance and scale human expertise and skills rather than replacing them. We therefore focus on practical applications of (AI) capabilities that assist people in performing well-defined tasks of needs by exploiting and wide range of (AI)-based services. We also use the term " cognitive computing" it is mean a comprehensive net of capabilities based on technology. It comprises the fields of machine learning, reasoning and decision technologies, language, speech and vision recognition and processing technologies, high performance and high efficient functions for any industries or individual consumers needs. For example, robotics, which are usually very good at doing what which are supposed to in any environment, much have public shopping center, factory etc. places which need simply services from the robot (machine man), such as cleans the floor of our houses to the robot that can work together with humans in production chains, passing through the warehouse, robots can take care of the tasks of an entire warehouse and the companion robots like Nao, Pepper, Aibo and Giraff, who can entertain use, talk to use and help elderly people to stay connected to their friends, relatives and doctors.

Google company is building automatic machine (self-driving cars) and has acquired more than 10 robotics companies. Facebook had opened whole new research facility only on (AI) research. Apply computer has developed Siri. Microsoft computer company has built a similar personalized assistant. Google has Deep mind, a UK company whose long term aim is to build general (AI) and has already great potential to win game to the world champion and IBM is investing a huge amount of resources in applying its Watson cognitive computing system to the medical domains to finance and to personalized education. In Europe, IBM is establishing new centers in Munich and Milan focused in the application of cognitive computer capabilities to the internet of things and healthcare respectively.

For example, automatic machine man (self-driving cars) are all about (AI), which used to be able to see what happens in the street (signals ,lanes, other cars, pedestrians, traffic lights, which need to able predict what other cars and pedestrians will do, and who need to be able to cope with unforeseen situations. Since, most car accidents are due to human fault, it is estimated that the adoption of self-driving cars will save about half of the lives that are usually last in car accidents.

IBM Watson company has to understand spoken language, make sense of massive amount to text , respond correctly to questions in many categories, as well as assess its own confidence in responding to such questions. In the future, (AI) technology can own question/answering capabilities that would be very useful, for example, in assisting a doctor when trying to some to the correct diagnosis for a patient and to propose the best therapy .

Intelligent machines can also rely on huge amounts of data to be used to learn how to make better decisions. This data comes from all of us over the years Facebook users have uploaded more than 250 billion pictures and every day who upload about 350 million more. Every second, we submit 40,000 google search queries. So, (AI) technology will be connected through the web from appliances to traffic lights from cars to watches. Other tasks that are very easy for humans are physical and manipulation tasks, such as walking , running, picking up an object to make its shape and location, restricted environment. But (AI) machine man technology still not able to have the general physical and manipulation capabilities even of a 6 year old.

So, it brings this question: Why do (AI) scientists need to concern ethics? Because (AI) technology is complex, information into insight has the potential to reveal long held secrets and help solve some of the world's most difficult problems. (AI) systems can potentially be used to help discover insights to treat disease, predict the whether, and manage the global economy. So, ethic issues is important to and (AI) scientists . If any one new (AI) technology research investigation could success, it will be a secret to and the (AI) scientists can not permit to their loyalty to any competitors to damage the fair (AI) technology products trading market. The country (countries) (AI) technology scientists need to concern ethic issues, who need to keep secrets for their countries economic or/and social benefits. This is moral issues to any countries/country loyalty is whose countries intangible assets. They can not sell (AI) loyalty to any their countries to assist whose economic benefits immorally.

● How can (AI) technology influence to global health care service needs?

According to (AI) lecturer analysis, when combined key clinical health (AI) application can potentially create $150 billion in annual savings for the US healthcare economy by 2026 year. (AI) technology is re-winning modern conception of healthcare delivery. It enables machines to sense, comprehend, act and learn. So which can perform administrative and clinical healthcare functions (Accenture, 2017).

It will help health care service organizations to reduce health care cost, will improve and raise service quality and access. So, (AI) health market size will be predicted growth. (AI) applications in health care include robot-assisted surgery, virtual nursing assistant, administrative workflow assistant, fraud detection, error reduction connected machines, clinical trial participant identifier, preliminary diagnosis, automated image diagnosis and cybersecurity.

What kind of benefits (AI) technology can contribute to healthcare service? (AI) technology can deliver what many health care organizations need, such as financial and operational of labor costs, digital expectations from patient consumers how to use (AI) technology to solve interoperability challenges in any healthcare organizations. Also (AI) technology can be applied to wellness an d lifestyle management, diagnostics, delivers financially but also way of organizational and workflow improvement. So, (AI) technology will be continue to become most prevalent and adoption to healthcare organizations , which must need to enhance structure to be position to take full advantages of new (AI) technological capabilities. (AI) technology can change the nature of work and employment is rapidly changing to make the best use of both humans and (AI) talent in healthcare industry in the future. For example, (AI) technology offers a way to fill in gaps and the rising labor shortage in healthcare. According to Accenture analysis, the physicians shortage is increasing. However, (AI) technology will manufacture healthcare machine men to replace physicians in future one day(2017). Hence, (AI) technology will be invented to raise health care service staffs work efficiency and performance in any hospitals or clinics in the future.

In conclusion, (AI) technology will raise efficiency for any service or manufacturing industries in the future, although, it is possible that it will also rise low skillful workers unemployment numbers. But, the most important influence to human technological innovation will be risen and it will influence human life will be changed to be better, e.g. self drive cars, health care physician machine men, machine man cleaners etc. intelligent machine men will be manufactured to serve for our daily life. Furthermore, (AI) technological products will influence countries trading, some low technological development countries manufacturing businessmen can choose to buy any (AI) products to raise whose productivity and efficiency and reducing cost to achieve economic cost saving result. Also, GDP of trading growth income will increase to the (AI) products sale countries. Hence, it will be beneficial to economic development to both developed and developing countries both in the future as well as (AI) scientists time and money spending will be valued to continue to invest (AI) technology development for human life and economy benefits for long term.

In conclusion (AI) technology will raise macro economy growth and it can create many (AI) jobs , but it also raise the low level technological worker unemployment change. In the future, (AI) technology can be applied to digital technology to attempt to invent any new undiscovered (AI) and digital technology. So, it needs any scientists to continue to research how digital and (AI) technology can be mixed to satisfy human's future undiscovered needs.

CHAPTER THREE

How robotics influence future tourism service market air ticket or e-ticket prebooking method change

I believe that applying (AI) big data tool to predict vehicle buyer consumption choice behavior, it is similar to predict traveler consumption choice behavior. In this chapter, I shall indicate how to apply (AI) big data gathering tool to predict vehicle buyer consumption choice behavior. Then, I shall its what its similar points to be applied to predict traveler consumption choice behavior. I believe that robotic can help tourism service industry to change future pre-book air ticket method.

Nowadays, many vehicle manufacturers hope their vehicles can attract to vehicle buyers to choose to buy their vehicles. However, there are many different brands of vehicles to provide to them to choose, so the vehicle market competition is very serious.

How to judge their different kinds of vehicle price which is reasonable acceptance to attract vehicle buyers to choose to buy the brand of vehicle manufacturers' any kinds of vehicles, e.g. fast speed sport style vehicles, comfortable and slow speed common cars, for four passengers common small size or more than four passengers common large car size?

How to evaluate the vehicle prices issue is important factor to influence vehicle buyers' choices. Either if the brand of vehicle price is too high to compare other brands of similar vehicle price, it will influence many vehicle buyers choose to buy other brands' vehicles or if the brand of vehicle price is too low, it will influence vehicle buyers feel this brand's vehicle machine quality or safe driving level or manufacturing steel material or speed or not comfortable sitting etc. different factors is worse to compare to other vehicle brands' similar vehicle products.

Thus, if the brand of vehicle manufacturers can predict how to design vehicles which can attract many vehicle buyers to choose to buy whose any vehicle products. What are future vehicle buyers' favorable vehicle styles? Then, the vehicle manufacturer can concentrate on manufacturing the kind style of vehicle products to sell already. It will reduce its vehicle manufacturing investment risk.

How to apply (AI) tools to predict vehicle buyers' behavioral consumption model? Whether artificial intelligent tools can predict automotive buyers' behavioral consumption model and predict future vehicle design trend. In fact, automotive brands and dealerships are facing an increasingly competition when attempting to manually gathering the vast quantities of data required to create customer focused programs that increase retention, ultimately new sales and service automotive business.

Building a based on that client's intrinsic needs and interests to any kinds of automotive vehicles at any given time. This is especially true in the automotive industry where the time span between purchases is measured in years. Because vehicle buyers would not like often to change their old vehicle to another new one. So, their decisions to buying another new vehicle, the time is usually after one year, even longer time. Hence, it seems any vehicles won't be frequent consumption products to the owned at least one vehicle family consumers (vehicle buyers). It implies that why vehicle manufacturers ought need to spend time to predict future vehicle buyer design choice for whole year vehicle buyer number growth because they won't often change preferable vehicle design to change another new vehicle more easily.

Hence, how to predict vehicle consumers' taste or preferable which styles of vehicle choices issues is very important. If the vehicle manufacturers can not manufacture any attractive vehicles to sell easily in this year. Then, it will lose time, money in this year because it won't know when the owned least one vehicle users or non-owned any vehicle users who will decide to buy one new vehicle or change another new vehicle ensure. The different brand vehicle dealers will possible wait more than one year to attract them to buy their vehicles if their styles are not attractive to compare other brands of vehicle competitors.

However, artificial intelligence and machine learning can help any vehicle manufacturers to find solution to solve patterns in highly to solve patterns in highly complex data-sets that are beyond the capability of a human brain, and then building and automatically acting on the customer insights it generates.

Given the automotive customer need for individualized communications, this technology is positioned to become a critical component of any successful vehicle retailer's domestic or/and overseas vehicle markets. How can vehicle manufacturers and retailers use (AI) to enhance their vehicle marketing campaigns? How will (AI) affect their vehicle sale marketing strategy? What criteria would they use when selecting on (AI) solution?

Vehicle consumers today are able to quickly access different brands of vehicle information, research vehicle products and reviews, negotiate prices and compare one vehicle brand or retailer to another resulting of the brands of vehicle customers. At the same time, the rise of " big -data mining", wearable devices that track user's every move and preference and greater contextualization in advertising and social media has resulted in consumer expectations of individualized. Thus, it seems that (AI) tools can be used to gather " big-data" and then they can make human's mind to analyze how to design kinds of vehicles to satisfy vehicle buyers' needs.

As automotive vehicle marketers can apply (AI) tools to achieve messaging strategies to meet the needs of this new generation of informed vehicle consumers, using data from a variety of sources to move from a variety of sources to move from mass- messaging to more personalized messages aimed at particular vehicle buyer segments, e.g. fast speed sport vehicle buyer segment, slow speed comfortable small size or large size of buyer segment. However, when 90% of vehicle marketers believe having a single vehicle buyer view is important, only 6% have achieved it.

However, one of the main issues vehicle marketers are facing the lack of capacity to efficiently sift through and analyze the massive vehicle buyer amounts of data required to create vehicle buyer individualized vehicle customer experiences easily. This is especially difficult for automotive dealers, the long periods between purchase cycles, and the highly considered nature of the vehicle purchase means that each vehicle dealer needs to not only track a large number of potential vehicle customers for an extremely long period of time, but each of those vehicle customers will generate a huge amount of different kinds of vehicle behavioral consumption data as they research their next vehicle purchase. However, by choosing the right (AI) technological tools and programs , vehicle dealers can solve this big data gathering challenge into a major advantage.

For Forrester vehicle brand example, vehicle consumers have more power over the Forrester vehicle brand's reputation than ever before. Mayne, L. (2014) indicated that Forrester calls this new (AI) tools is the " age of the vehicle customer", a 20 year business cycle in which the most successful vehicle enterprises will reinvent themselves to systematically understand and serve increasingly powerful vehicle consumers. To win in this new age, Forrester declares companies must become vehicle customer obsessed and the only sustainable competitive advantage is knowledge and engagement with customers, such as (AI) gathering data knowledge.

Thus, the biggest challenge vehicle businesses currently face is not the collection of a large quantity of vehicle consumer data, but what to do with that data once they have it. Even at a large vehicle data research firm, the data sets are often too big for a single analyze, or even a team of analysts to sort through and draw conclusion from. However, enter artificial intelligence and machine learning , an efficient technology solution that can continuously find patterns in highly complex data sets that are way beyond the capacity of a human brain and then automatic drive action based on the customer insights is generated.

What is (AI) machine learning tool? Machine learning is a type of (AI) that learns from data and is not explicitly program. Think Amazon, face book. Machine learning serves up relevant content based on an individual vehicle purchase behavior and experiences. More simply, machine learning is a computer program that can learn relationships between data, subject those learnings to errors functions, and then learn from its errors. The program in effect, trains itself.

Lee, T. (2016) explained that "Thus, (AI) tools can learn deep a more advanced branch of machine learning inspired by how our brain's nervous function, has also been found to be especial effective in identifying patterns from data."

When this way sound is complicated from a vehicle dealer perspective, the implementation of a marketing program driven by artificial intelligence can take care of these tasks in an automatic vehicle fashion with little to no manual intervention required from the staff at time vehicle stores.

In practice at a vehicle dealership, the program will continue track vehicle customer behavior online, merging that data with any offline source (like CRM or DMS data) and then analyze this aggregated vehicle buyer data set to predict what vehicle customer may be shopping for and what information they might like to relevance from different kinds style of vehicle design photos.

● Robotic can assist taxi or air ticket buyers to raise pre-booking taxi or air ticket service efficiency

Artificial intelligence refers to complex in vehicle market and travelling entertainment market which is very seem to be applied to predict consumer behaviors.

(AI) machine learning that posses the same characteristics of human intelligence and that have all our sense, all our reason and think just like human vehicle buyer who prefer vehicle purchase choice or travelling consumer who prefer travelling package or travelling destination and airline choice. Besides, machine learning is the practice of using algorithms to collect and examine data, learn from it, and then make a determination or prediction about something in the world.

So, it can be attempted to gather data concerns that travelling consumer past travelling destination choice and air ticket price choice and different travelling package, e.g. high, middle, or low class hotel and foods supply and entertainment places choice in their past travelling journeys.

The machine is " trained" using large amounts of data and algorithms that give it the ability to learn how to automatically perform a task with increasing accuracy. Otherwise, deep learning is primarily based on artificial neural networks inspired by our understanding of the biology of human's brains.

Thus, (AI) big data can gather all these past traveler consumption behavioral choice data to make reference to analyze whether how many travelers will choose to go to the specific travelling destination in any time by the past traveler number record to different travelling destinations, then it can gather the past air ticket sale price to different destinations and past travelling package design to different destinations in order to analyze whether it is the cheap airline ticket price factor or attractive travelling package factor or attractive travelling entertainment etc. in order to predict which factor is the most potential influential factor to they choose to go to the destination to travel in different time within one year. Then, traveler agent or airline can collect these big data to judge how to design their package to attract travelers to go to anywhere to travel or what the main factor influence most of them to choose to visit the destination to travel.

For example, travel agents or airlines can apply "Deep learning" breaks down tasks in ways that enables machines to assist them to predict when travelling consumer choice will be changed and why their travelling choice will change and how their travelling choice will change with increasingly complex tasks.

So, such as why (AI) technology can be applied to predict how travelling consumer behavior changes to bring to judge whether anywhere will be many travelling consumers who will prefer to choose travelling hot destinations next year or next month.

Then, travel agents and airlines can gather overall past travelling consumer data to analyze and conclude the more accurate prediction of different travelling destinations to the number of traveler. Then, they can choose how much air ticket price is more reasonable to charge to the travelling destination or how to design the travelling package which can bring more attractive to the prediction number of different travelling destination travelers in order to achieve to raise the different travelling destination number next year.

Thus, (AI) big data machine learning can help airlines or travel agents to solve how to design any attractive travelling package challenge. A travelling package is both one of the most important and carefully considered travelling entertainment consumption the majority of travelling people will ever make in their lifetime at least one travelling time.

It is also a prediction how travelling package will be designed that tends to be fundamentally tied to a travelling person's travelling destination choice identify and travelling package view of themselves. As the same time, travelling consumers' travelling choice changing lifestyles result in changing travelling destination needs, e.g. the country's young travelers can choose to change non-extreme exciting travelling entertainment package from past extreme exciting travelling entertainment package. Due to personal feeling factor in general. However, I believe that (AI) big data can also be attempted to predict when the country's young travelers will choose to change non-extreme exciting travelling behavior.

It is similar to automotive dealers need to remember that vehicle customers and prospects are individual human beings with risk, complex and ever-changing lives factors, these factors will influence every vehicle consumer why who feels has vehicle purchase need, and how who choose to buy the first vehicle if who decided to buy the first vehicle.

It seems that travelling agents or airlines need to remember that travelling consumers and different features or designs are very traveler beings with risk, complex and ever-travelling package attitude personal changing factors in different travel season, these factor will influence every individual traveler why who feels has travel entertainment need, and how who choose to buy different feature or design travelling package if who decide to travel. The (AI) big data technological travelling customer behavioral prediction tool seems to be the best travelling behavioral prediction tool in the world are those that know every one of different country's traveler need. Their likes and dislikes which style of travelling package, preferences and travel destination changing tastes to travelling destination choices.

The capacity of the human brain, however, limits us from achieving these different type of travel package sales. In this competitive travelling destination choice entertainment environment, (AI) big data machine learning enables platforms to assist the air ticket and travel package sales team by tracking the travelling consumer behaviors of each travelling customer, learning and memorizing their preferences and predicting their future travelling destination choice and travelling package design needs.

Finally, I recommend that for a travel agent or airline travelling marketing platform to make their travelling customer engagement efficient and fully-functional, I should be able to: applying (AI) tools to track every travelling customer behavior across the web, connecting to a society of data sources, CRM, DMS, third-party, web travelling brands, social traveler email, click etc., aggregating and accurately cross-reference data from a variety of sources, leveraging this data to drive insights on a mass scale, as well as on an individualized basis, driving actions and automatically direct travelling customer engagement via multiple channels based on where each customer is in their travelling individual lifecycle.

Why is (AI) big data gathering tool better than psychological and survey methods to predict traveler individual travel choice behavior?

Prediction travel behavioral consumption from psychology and survey methods.

How to predict travel consumption? It is one question to any travel agents concern to use what methods which can predict how many numbers of travelers where who will choose to go to travel more accurately. I think that who can consider how to predict travel behavioral consumption from psychology and survey travel choice prediction method, but it is better to apply (AI) big data gathering method to predict travel consumer's destination choice more accurate. The reason is as below:

The first reason is that traveller individual travel psychological desire is difficult to predict accurate more than (AI) big data gathering method, it is due that the data is past traveler's destination choice and travel package and ticket price actual data from (AI) big data gathering method. Otherwise, survey investigation is only traveler psychological thinking method. It lacks enough past actual traveler data gathering.

The second reason is that on the weakness of traveler individual psychological thinking view of survey investigation. It has evidence to support the relationship between self-identify threat and resistance to change travel behavior to any travelers, controlling for whose past travelling behavior, resistance to change if a psychological phenomenon of long standing interest in many applied branches of psychology.

Past travelling behavior has been acknowledged as a predictor of future action. Such as travelling behavior that is experienced as successful is likely to be repeated and may lead to habitual patterns. Some psychologists differentiate habit between two concepts, such as goal oriented and automatic oriented both. Although repeated past travelling behavior is addition goal oriented and automatic oriented. Further non-deliberative nature of habit may make appeals to judge and to predict future individual traveler's behavior accurately.

However, repeated one traveler will choose the destination to repeat to travel without a necessary constraint of goal orientation and automatic oriented both. So, it seems that psychological factor can influence any individual traveler why and how who choose to decide to repeat to choose the destination to travel.

So, survey investigation is only the traveler's thinking to answer the travel firm. It is not sure that the traveler's past travel experience is real answer. Otherwise, (AI) big data gathering method is computer gathering method which gather past traveler consumption actual data to analyze and conclude future traveler possible repeated travel destination choice and travel package choice more accurate.

The third reason is that on the strength of (AI) big data gathering method computer statistic view to predict future traveller consumer's destination and travel package choice. It is structural equation modeling is an extremely flexible linear-in-parameters multivariate statistical modeling technique. It has been used in modeling travel behavior and values since about 1980 year. It is a software method to handle a large number of variables, as well as unobserved variables specified as linear combinations (weighted averages) of the observed variable.

1.3 Can (AI) big data gather data to predict when climate will change to influence poor travelling behaviours?

(AI) big data tool can predict the flexibility of human travelling behavioral change is at least the result of one such mechanism, our ability to travel mentally in time and entertain potential future. Understanding of the impacts is holidays, particularly those involving travel.

Using focus groups research to explores tourists' awareness of the impacts of travel own climate change, examines the extent to which climate change features in holiday travel decisions and identifies some of the barriers to the adoption of less carbon intensive tourism practices.

The findings suggest many tourists don't consider climate change when planning their holidays. The failure of tourists to engage with the climate change to impact of holidays, combined with significant barriers to behavioral change, presents a considerable challenge in the tourism industry. In the future, computer (AI) big data tool can attempt to predict when the country's climate change to influence travelers to choose to go to the country to travel, e.g. next month or next half year or next year hot travelling destinations.

Tourism is a highly energy intensive industry and has only recently attracted attention as an important contributions to climate change through greenhouse gas emissions. It has been estimated that tourism contributes 5% of global carbon dioxide emissions. There have been a number of potential changes proposed for reducing the impact of air travel on climate change. These include technological changes, market based changes and behavioral changes.

However, the role that climate change plays in the holiday and travel decisions of global tourists. How the global tourists of the impacts travel has on climate change to establish the extent to which climate change, considerations features in holiday travel decision making processes and to investigate the major barriers to global tourists adopting less carbon intensive travel practices.

It will bring this question: Will tourists aware the impacts that their holidays and travel have on climate changes to influence their travelling decision?

When, it comes to understand individual traveler's behavioral change, wide range of conceptual theories have been developed, utilizing various social, psychological, subjective and objective variables in order to model travel consumption behavior. These theories of travel behavioral change operate at a number of different levels, including the individual level, the interpersonal level and community level. Whether pro-environmental behavior can be used to predict travel consumption behavior in a climate change. However, the question of what determines pro-environmental behavior in such a complex one that it can not be visualized through one single framework or diagram.

Despite the potentially high risk scenario for the tourism industry and the global environment, the tourism and climate change ought have close relationship.

However, (AI) big data tool can be applied to find what factors to influence the time of travelers' travelling choices. What are the important factors and variables which can limit tourism? e.g. money, time, family problem, extreme hot or cold weather change, air ticket price, journey attraction etc. variable factors.

Mention of holidays and travel were deliberately avoided in the recruitment process, so as not to create a connection factor to influence traveler's individual mind. However, the dismissal of alternative transportation modes can be conceived as either a structural barrier, in the sense that flying is perhaps the only realistic option to reach long-haul holiday destination, or a perceived behavioral control barriers in that an individual perceives flying as the only option open to whom.

The transportation tool factor will be depend to extent on the distance to the destination. This can also be interpreted in a social perspective as an intention with the resources available where much international tourism is structured around flying. To increase the availability of different transportation modes, tourists could choose holiday destination closer to home.

Finally, also how to predict future travel behavioral consumption. I feel that travel agents need to predict whether any country's random daily variation of weather factor is also important to influence travel behavior. e.g. in weather, temperature, rainfall and snowfall with traffic accidents factors will have relationship to cause travel demand.

Some scientists estimate suggest that when warmed temperatures and reduced snowfall are associated with a moderate decline in non-fatal accidents, they are also associated with a significant increase in fatal accidents. Thus increase in fatalities and temperature. Half of the estimated effect of temperature on fatalities is due to changes in the exposure to pedestrians, bicyclists and motorcyclists as temperature increase.

So, if any countries have rainfall, snowfall and low temperature to cause traffic accidents, whether this accident occurrence will influence the travelers who liking climb snow hills, riding bicycle, running sports who will avoid to travel to these countries' bad weather after occurs. So, why I feel that this natural climate factor will also be one serious factor to influence travel behavioral consumption. However, (AI) big data tool can predict more accurate than survey method when climate change to influence the country's climate to be poor, then it can predict when which countries are not popular acceptable to global country consumers' travel choice next month.

How can apply (AI) to provide travelling businesses with better-informed decisions ?

I shall explain how (AI) big data gathering technology can provide travelling businesses with better-informed decisions to drive top-line growth, deliver meaningful experience for travelling customers and smooth their path along the travelling consumer journey. The widely understood definition of (AI) involves the ability of machines or computers to learn human thinking, reasoning and decision-making abilities.

So, such as (AI) learning machine system can attempt to learn travelling consumer's travel destination or travel package thinking, judgement of their reasons why they choose to go to the destination to travel or why they choose to buy the travel package and learn how and why they make their past travelling decisions from their past travel big data gathering.

A Narrative science study in 2015 year identified that (AI) was being used primarily in voice recognition, machine learning virtual assistants and decision support. This study also highlighted the many branches of (AI) and that techniques and their definition are used interchangeably. It is possible that (AI) can be used to gather big data , then to analyze to help travel businesses to predict travelling consumer travel destination and travel package choice behaviors. For example, one of the most common techniques is traveler machine learning, where algorithms are used to perform tasks by learning from the airline or travel agent whose past all travelers' travelling destination choice and travel package choice historical data.

However, during 2017 year, search engines will begin to find what additional factors can influence past traveler personal travelling destination and travelling package travelling behavioral data into prediction of future travelling customer behavioral results, such as the online traveler (user's) history of travelling data searches, such as anywhere are the most popular travelling locations or travelling destinations and previously captures conservations.

Artificial intelligence will use this past travelling destinations and travelling package information to power predictive search results, e.g. predictive future travelling consumer's choice behavioral processing for where will be their preferable travelling destination choice and how to design travelling package to satisfy future travelling clients' needs.

Predictive search will improve the quality of online travelling search results, and provide new insights into travelling consumers' travelling destination and package behavior and the moments which matter to them. Search will give recommendation into tailored how travelling consumer individual travelling destination choice in travelling decision making process. Several of the largest online platforms already use (AI) travelling machine learning to improve predictive travelling consumer behavioral search results.

For example, Google's rank brain technology adds research by understanding the context in which the travelling consumer has entered it. Over time, rank brain will learn further from user behaviors Amazon's DSSTNE (pronouned destiny) learns from shoppers' purchasing habits and consumption behavior to offer better product recommend actions, which Amazon can offer before a consumer has entered anything into the search bar.

Such as (AI) big data can gather past online travelers' e-ticket purchase transactions to conclude that online traveler's travelling choice habits and online traveler consumption behavior to offer better travelling destinations and travelling package opinions to travel agents or airlines. However, this technology is not independent of human input. For example, Google engineers will periodically retain the rank brain system to improve the models it uses.

For another example, in 2016 year , Apple computer revamped its travelling scene photos app to allow travelling consumers to search for specific travelling destinations in the travelling scene phots, they want to find anywhere travelling destination photos, not just dates and locations. Each travelling photo that an intelligent phone or intelligent pad user takes goes through 11 billion computations, so that travelling scene photos can understand exactly where is the travelling destination photography to let online travelling consumer to feel anywhere they plan to go to the location to travel. So, (AI) learning machine can make online travelling photos more attractive to influence potential travelers choose to the destination to travel after they see the travelling destination scene photos from internet.

It seems that in future, (AI) machine learning will allow online travelling search to evolve even further. Search engineers will deliver refined recommendations to airlines' online traveler e-ticket search users and use less human input to predict travelling consumers' needs from internet channel. For IBM computer example, it indicated 90% of the data that exists today has been created in the last two years.

This huge explosion of past traveler's e-ticket consumption data gives the opportunity to quickly spot and react to the latest trends, fashion and fads among its travelling clients and potential clients. This will allow airline or travel agent companies to better engage with younger travelling consumers, who gain influence access to the latest travelling destination and package trends.

They associate with to help define who they are as individuals. Thus, travelling company brands have to identify and make use of them before travelling consumers move on, but the vast quantity of past e-ticket purchase data available makes from internet channel. This a resource-intensive task. For next example, Lesara, a based online clothes store, uses this machine learning to inform its product decision often gathering information from internal and external sources.

When its trends -spotting shoes. Lesara has a range of over 20 styles and sells hundreds of pairs a day. It focus on giving consumers, the very latest trends allow Lesara to develop on average of 50,000 new items each year. It compared to 11,000 old items each year. Thus, travelling agents or airlines can attempt to apply (AI) big data gathering method to gather all past e-ticket purchase data, concerns where they prefer to choose to go to the destinations to travel and what travelling packages are the most attractive to the travelers to choose to buy. It aims to help them to predict where future travelers will prefer to choose to go to travel or what travelling package they will prefer to choose to buy next year.

For another (AI) big data prediction example, Lesara is one online clothes store, uses machine learning decisions after gathering information from internal and external sources. One of its most popular products, shoes with LED started life when its trend spotting software flagged up a blogger wearing similar shoes. Now Lesara has a range of over 20 styles and sells hundreds of pairs a day. Its focus on giving consumers the very latest trends allows Lesara to develop an average of 50,000 new items each year, compared to 11,000 for its competitor Lara.

It seems (AI) big data gathering machine learning can help Lesara business to predict what kinds of shoes design or style that shoe consumers will prefer choose to buy in future shoe market trend. Thus, Lesara can predict shoe consumers' taste successfully and it can manufacture many attractive style of shoes.

(AI) machine learning can gather global past shoe consumer's shoe shopping experiences, then analyzes to make conclusion to give lesara recommendation successfully. This will make the experience more enjoyable for shoe consumers and allow Lesara to advert whose different new style or design of shoes to deliver them move relevant messages by understanding the context of the experience.

So, online travel agents or online airline can also attempt to apply (AI) big data gathering method to predict where travelers will prefer to go to travel and how they ought design travelling packages to attract them to choose to buy next year. Hence, (AI) big data gathering technology can conclude how to design traveler agents' travelling package products to be the most attractive to excite many travelers choose to buy their travelling package, due to it has more accurate to predict travelling consumer destination and travelling package choice behaviors to compare human themselves prediction judgement effort, e.g. travelling survey or marketing research, or telephone enquire. It seems that (AI) machine judgement effort is more accurate to compare to human judgment effort in travelling industry.

Future travel consumption behavior

Can (AI) big data gathering tool predict traveler individual habitual behavior , e.g. renting travel transportation tools ?

Can (AI) big data gathering tool can predict past traveler destination and travelling package choice habit and it can be intended to predict of future traveler behavior to people are creatures of habits judgement of future anywhere travelling destination choice next year or next month or next half year destination prediction ?

Many of human's everyday goal-directed behaviors are performed in a habitual fashion, the transportation made and route one takes to work, one's choice of breakfast. Habits are formed when using the some behavior frequently and a similar consistency in a similar context for the some purpose whether the individual past travel consumption model will be caused a habit to whom. e.g. choosing whom travel agent to buy air ticket or traveling package; choosing the same or similar countries' destinations to go to travel ; choosing the business class or normal (general) class of quality airlines to catch planes.

Does habitual rent traveling car tools use not lead to more resistance to change of travel mode? It has been argued that past behavior is the best predictor of future behavior to travel consumption. If individual traveler's past consumption behavior was always reasoned, then frequency of prior travel consumption behavior should only have an indirect link to the individual traveler's behavior. It seems that renting travel car tools to use is a habit example. So, a strong rent traveling car tools useful habit makes traveling mode choice. People with a strong renting of traveling car tools of habit should have low motivation to attend to gather any information about public transportation in their choice of travelling country for individual or family or friends members during their traveling journeys.

Even when persuasive communication changes the traveler whose attitudes and intention, in the case of individual traveler or family travelers with a strong renting travel car tools habit. It is difficult to change whose travel behaviors to choose to catch public transportation in whose any trips in any countries. However, understanding of travel behavior and the reasons for choosing one mode of transportation over another. The arguments for rent traveling car tools to use, including convenience, speed, comfort and individual freedom and well known.

Increasingly, psychological factors include such as, perceptions, identity, social norms and habit are being used to understand travel mode choice. Whether how many travel consumers will choose to rent traveling car tools during their trips in any countries. It is difficult to estimate the numbers. As the average level of renting travel car tools of dependence or attitudes to certain travel package policies from travel agents. Instead different people must be treated in different ways because who are motivated in different ways and who are motivated by different travel package policies ways from travel agents.

In conclusion, the factors influence whose traveler's individual traveler destination choice behavior The factors include either who chooses to rent traveling car tools or who chooses to catch public transportation when who individual goes to travel in alone trip or family trip. It include influence mode choice factors, such as social psychology factor and marketing on segmentation factor both to influence whose transportation choice of behavior in whose trip. So, (AI) big data can be attempted to gather past traveler transportation tool choice, rent travelling car tools choice or catching public transportation tools choice to predict where destination can provide what kind of transportation tool to attract many travelers to choose to go to the place to travel.

How (AI) big data determine future travel behavior from past travel experience and perceptions of risk and safety for the benefits to travel consumers?

How (AI) big data determine future travel behavior from past travel experience and perceptions of risk and safety for the benefits to travel consumers? Why does individual traveler avoid certain destination(s) is(are) as relevant to tourist decision making as why who chooses to travel to others?

Perceptions of risk and safety and travel experience are likely to influence travel decisions. If travel agents had efforts to predict future travel behavior to guess whether travelers will feel where is(are) risk and unsafe to cause who does not choose to go to the country to travel. Then, the travel agents will avoid to choose to spend much time to design the different traveling package to attract their potential travel consumers to choose to travel. The reason is because in the case of individual traveler's tourism experience, the traveler whose past disappointment travel experience (psychological risk) will be a serious threat to the traveler's health or life (health, physical or terrorism risk). The past safety or unhealthy risk to the country(countries) will influence the traveler decides to choose not to go to the countries(country) to travel again in the future.

What is push and pull factors to influence any traveler who chooses where is whose preferable travelling destination ?

How to apply (AI) big data to predict individual traveler's behavioral intention of choosing a travel destination?

Understanding why people travel and what factors influence their behavioral intention of choosing a travel destination is beneficial to tourism planning and marketing. In general, an individual's choice of a travel destination into two forces.

The first force is the push factor that pushes an individual away from home and attempt to develop a general desire to go somewhere, without specifying where that may be.

The other force is the pull factor that pull an individual toward in destination, due to a region-specific or perceived attractiveness of a destination. The respective push and pull factors illustrate that people travel because who are pushed by whose internal motives and pulled by external forced of a destination. However, the decision making process leading to the choice of a travel destination is a very complex process.

For example, a Taiwanese traveler who might either choose new travel destination of Hong Kong or another old travel Asia destinations again or who also might choose any one of Western country, as a new travel destination. The travel agents can predict where who will have intention to choose to travel from whose past behavior and attitude, subjective and perceived behavioral control model. When (AI) big data gather past every country traveler number who chose to go to which countries to travel in order to judge where destinations will be the country travelers' travelling choice destinations in the future.

The factors influence where is the traveler choice, include personal safety, scenic beauty, cultural interest, climate changing, transportation tools, friendliness of local people, price of trip, trip package service in hotels and restaurants, quality and variety of food and shopping facilities and services etc. needs. So, whose factors will influence where is the individual travel's choice. It seems every traveler whose choice of travel process, will include past behavior. e.g. travelling experience, travelling habit, then to choose the best seasoned travelling action to satisfy whose travel needs. This process is the individual traveler's psychological choice process, who must need time to gather information to compare concerning of different travel packages, destination scene, climate change, transportation tools available to the destination, air ticket price etc. these factors, then to judge where is the best right destination to travel in the right time.

Hence, (AI) big data can gather past different countries' climate changing data, transportation tool changing data, destination scene environment changing etc. different data to give opinions to travelling businesses whether any country's these above factors will influence about how many traveler number will be increase or decrease in the future.

Why can expectation, motivation and attitude factor influence travelling behavior?

Social psychology is concerned with gaining insight into the psychological of socially relevant behaviors and the processes. For instance, on a global level bad influence to global warming, it influences some countries extreme cold or hot bad climate changing occurrence, then it ought influence some travelers' behavioral decision to change their mind to choose some countries to go to travel at the moment which do not occur extreme hot or cold climate (temperature). e.g. above than 40 degree in summer or below than 0 degree in winter. Due to the extreme climate changing environment in the countries, it will cause them to feel uncomfortable to play during their trips. So, the global warming causes to climate changing factor will influence the numbers of travel consumption to be reduced possibly. This is global climate changing environment factor influences to bad or uncomfortable social psychological feeling to global travelers' mind of traveling decision. What is individual traveler expectation, motivation and attitude? Tourism sector includes inbound (domestic) tourism and outbound (overseas) tourism both incomes to any countries. According to recent article, a tourist behavior model has been developed, called the expectation, motivation and attitude (EMA) model (Hsu et al., 2010).

This model focuses on the pre-visit stage of tourists by modeling the behavioral process by incorporating expectation, motivation and attitude. Travel motivation is considered as an essential component of the behavioral process, which has been increasing attention from the travel; industry. The economic approach defines "tourism" is an identifiable nationally important industry. It includes the component activities of transportation, accommodation, recreation, food and related service. So, tourism behavioral consumption is concerned the individual tourist's usual habituate of the industry which responds to whose needs, and of the impacts that both the tourist and the tourism industry have on the socio-cultural, economic and physical environment.

However, travel motivation means how to understand and predict factors that influence travel decision making. According to Backman and others (1995, p.15), motivation is conceptually viewed as " a state of need, a condition that services as a driving force to display different kind of behavior toward certain types of activities, developing preferences, arriving at some expected satisfactory outcome." So, motivation and expectancy which has close relationship to any tourist before who decided to do any tourism of behavior.

Some economists confirmed motivation and expectancy which has relations, such as expectation of visiting an outbound destination has a direct effect on motivation to visit the destination; motivation has a direct effect on attitude toward visiting the destination; expectation of visiting the outbound destination has a direct affection on attitude toward visiting the destination and motivation has a mediating effect on the relationship in between expectation and attitude.

Hence, (AI) big data can gather all the country's climate environment change, transportation tool change, entertainment scene change, hotel price and restaurant price change etc. data to give opinions whether the country will attract how many traveler to choose to go to travel in the year.

What is (AI) deep learning techniques to forecast travelling environment behavioral consumption

Prediction how many travelers will choose to go to the country to travel. It is similar to apply deep-learning technology to predict how to raise the agricultural farming productivity in the agricultural export country.

The (AI) deep-learning technology leads to performance enhancement and generalization of artificial intelligent technology. It influences the global leader in the field of information technology has declared its intention to utilize the deep-learning technology to solve environmental problems, such as climate change.

So, it will help agriculture farming businesses can raise any plant food: vegetable, fruit, rice which grow up very easily if farmers can apply (AI) deep-learning technology to solve environment problems to influence their plant food grow. If the whole year seasonal change is very good and it is suitable for any plant food to grow in farming land easily, e.g. rain is enough and soil is enough for any plant food to grow in the farm lands. Then, fruit, rice, vegetable etc. agriculture businesses will have much beneficial attribution to global farmers.

The question is how to use deep-learning technologies in the environmental field to predict the status of pro-environmental consumption. We predicted the pro-environmental consumption index based on Google search query data, using a recurrent neural network (RNN model). To certify the accuracy of the index, we compared the prediction accuracy of the RNN model with that of the ordinary least square and artificial necessary network models.

For example, the RNN model predicts the pro-environmental consumption index better than any other model. we expect the RNN model to perform still better in a big data environment because the deep-learning technologies would be increasingly as the volume of data grows. So, deep-learning technologies could be useful in environmental forecasting to prevent damage caused by climate change to influence any rice, vegetable, tomato, potato, fruit etc. different plant food grow in any countries' farming land easily.

For South Korea example, over 800 government agencies spent 2.2 trillion Korea won on eco-products in 2014 year. However, green products are rarely purchased outside these agencies. This phenomenon occurs because there is a gap between consumer attitudes and behavior , that is environmental attitude is a major factor in decision making vis-a-vis the consumption of " green" food and services (Jorea Ministry of Environment, 2015).

Therefore, it is necessary to understand those consumer attitude, that will lead to sustainability-conductive behavior and consumption. (AI) Deep learning system can be applied to attempt understand those traveler attitude to environment protection to fly to which country. For example, (AI) deep learning system can attempt to gather data concerns how many Hong Kong people concern air pollution challenge to influence their health, then it can attempt to predict how many Hong Kong travelers do not choose to go China travel, due to the air pollution challenge to influence their health.

● How roboics can attact many travellers choose natural environment travelling package

Recently, many researchers have studied pro-environmental consumption and household indexes as well as suicide rate predictions using messages posted by internet users on Google trend, Tweets etc. channel.

Whether can environmental consumption be predicted by (AI) deep-learning technological internet channel to influence how many travelers choose to go to the country to travel?

How can impact the pro-environmental consumption attitudes of green policies to influence how many travelers choose to go to the country to travel?

For example, Korea scientists estimated pro-environmental attitudes using search query data provided by Google trend and confirmed through regression analysis, that pro-environmental attitude has a positive correlation with the pro-environmental attitude index. They also explained that environment-friendly attitude of residents plan an important role in policy making. In the past, most household consumption indexed were calculated through surveys, but (AI) deep-learning technological tool " big data" have recently gained research attention (Lee et al. 2016). So, (AI) deep learning technology can attempt to gather whether how many Korea residents who concern environment pollution to influence their eating green food attitude then to judge whether how many Korea residents hope to leave their country to travel anywhere either high risk environment pollution countries to travel or low risk environment pollution countries to travel in the future.

It seems that (AI) deep-learning technology can help agricultural export countries' farmers , e.g. US, UK, Canada, New Zealand, Australia, Japan, China, India etc. they can predict environmental behavioral consumption to any rice, tomato, potato , fruit, vegetable etc. plant food consumers. The beneficial advantages to them include as below:

(a) Assuming they know their countries' weather, when it has less rain to cause drought or when it has more rain in any seasonal time in the year. They can choose not to grow any kinds of above these plant food to avoid loss.

(b) They can make any kinds of above these plant food price raising after their prediction of these bad seasonal time to cause their plant food shortage supply challenge. Because these plant food consumers' demand number is more, but the supply of these above plant food supply number is less. However, due to they had predicted when the bad seasonal time can not allow them to grow these above plant food before. So, they have enough time to grow many these above plant food number in predictive good seasonal time to prepare to supply to their plant food import countries' plant food consumers to eat. Thus, these predictive environmental consumption plant food export countries can raise their plant food price to sell to them. When, the other non-pre-predictive environmental consumption plant food export countries can not supply any one of those plant food to them to eat, due to the bad climate to cause them can't grow any one of these plant food to export to sell.

Thus, (AI) deep-learning technology can be applied to predict how to raise the plant food supply number in order to raise price to the import plant food countries consumers to eat, due to they feel difficult to buy these plant food to eat in the bad climate seasonal time in whole year.

(c) (AI) deep-learning technology can help climate scientists to find what reasons cause their countries; rain sudden increases or cause their countries' rain sudden decreases. After its gathering data analysis, it can assist climate scientists to find solution methods to attempt to control the rain level can be right falling down level to let agricultural export farmers who can grow their plant food to sell to agricultural import countries in whole year.

(d) The agricultural export countries' farmers can apply (AI) deep-learning technology to help them to choose whether growing which kinds of plant food in that whether climate time to earn more plant food consumption number more easily.

Due to the agricultural countries climate will often change, for example, tomato, potato, rice, fruit etc. plant food can be adapt to grow in more rain time, but vegetable can not be adapt to grow in more rain time. If farmers can apply this technology to predict when it will have move rain or when it will have less rain to fall down in their countries. Then, they can choose to grow which kinds of plant food number more, in the suitable seasonal climate time in order to raise plant food growing number productivities to supply to sell to satisfy any agricultural food import countries' demand effectively.

(e) (AI) deep-learning technology can help agricultural import countries to solve agricultural food shortage challenge in long term. When this technology can be popular to base applied by the agricultural plant food export countries. It will solve global agricultural food shortage challenge. For example, when one agricultural export countries' farmers can popular accept to apply this technology to predict when to grow which kinds of plant food more to rise number productivities to sell. e.g. vegetable, fruit, rice Besides another agricultural export countries' farmers can also accept to apply this technology to predict when to grow plant food, e.g. potato, tomato to raise number productivities to sell. Then, they can concentrate on growing the specific kinds of plant food in order to raise the specific plant food number productivities in every seasonal change time every month. Then, global agricultural plant food supply must be raised, due to these predictive environmental change farmers can know who ought grow which kinds of plant food to sell to raise number productivities.

Consequently, (AI) deep learning can gather where countries will have high risk environment pollution to influence health food supply. Then, it can give opinions to travelling businesses when these high risk environment pollution countries will encounter the traveler number to be decreased, due to the environment pollution serious challenge will occur.

How to use qualitative of travel behavioral method to predict future travel consumption from (AI) big data ?

I also suggest to use qualitative of travel behavioral method to predict future travel consumption. Methods such as focus groups interviews and participant observer techniques can be used with quantitative approaches on their own to fill the gaps left by quantitative techniques. These insights have contributed to the development of increasingly sophisticated models to forecast travel behavior and predict changes in behavior in response to change in the transportation system. I shall indicate the weaknesses of human travelling investigation methods as below:

First, survey methods restrict not only the question frame but the answer frame as well, anticipating the important issues and questions and the responses. However, these surveys methods are not well suited to exploratory areas of research where issues remain unidentified and the researched seek to answer the question "why?".

Second, data collection methods using traditional travel diaries or telephone recruitment can under represent certain segments of the population, particularly the older persons with little education, minorities and the poor. Before the survey, focus group for example can be used to identify what socio-demographic variables to include in the survey, how best to structure the diary, even what incentives will be most effective in increasing the response rate.

After the survey, focus, focus groups can be used to build explanations for the survey results to identify the "why" of the results as well as the implications. One Asia Pacific survey research result was made by tourism market investigation before. It indicated the travel in Asia Pacific market in the past, had often been undertaken in large groups through leisure package sold in bulk, or in large organized business groups, future travelers will be in smaller groups or alone, and for a much wider range of reasons.

Significant new traveler segments, such as female business traveler. The small business traveler and the senior traveler, all of which have different aspirations and requirements from the travel experience.

Moreover, Asia tourism market will start to exist behaviors in the adoption of newer technologies, a giving the traveler new ways to manage the travel experience, creating new behaviors. This with provide new opportunities for travel providers. The use of mobile devices, smartphones, tablets etc. and social media are the obvious findings to become an integral part of the travel experience. Thus, quality method can attempt to predict Asia Pacific tourism market development in the future. It is such as (AI) big data gathering tool can give traveler quality opinions to any travelling businesses to make the more accurate where will be the popular travel destination choice next month or next half year or next year.

However, improving the predictive power of travel behavior models and to increase understanding travel behavior which lies in the use of panel data(repeated measures from the same individuals). Whereas, cross-sectional data only reveal inter-individual differences at one moment in time, panel data can reveal intra-individual changes over time. In effect, panel data are generally better suited to understand and predict (changes in) travel behavior. However, a substantial proportion was also observed to transition between very different activity/travel patterns over time, indicating that from one year to the next, many people renegotiated their activity/travel patterns.

How to apply advanced traveler information systems (ATIS) to predict future travelling behavior?

Nowadays, information can impact on traveler behavior and network performance. For example, when steadily growing levels of vehicle ownership and vehicle miles traveled information has been identified as a potential strategy towards man aging travel demand, optimizing transportation networks and better utilizing available capacity. Toward, this goal to predict further tourist behavioral consumption. Many countries, government tourism development institutes has applied advanced traveler information systems (ATIS) which travel behavior models and high-fidelity network performance models made increasingly feasible through the rapid advances in computer power. Crucial components of this problem domain are the modeling of individual tourist drivers' response to travel information and the development accurate guidance of relevance to real would trip makers. So, this advanced traveler information systems (ATIS) can assist the tourist who like to rent travelling car tools to travel in any countries own free traveler information systems service conveniently. Also, this travel information system can be intended to assist travelers to make better travel choices. e.g. this system can improve the decision making of individual traveler rather than improvements of network performance overall. So, we need to understand how tourists make their travel plans. Also, understanding decision process that lead to booking of the trip is equally important, as it allows of a potential behavior.

How can online tourism sale channel influence natural environment traveling consumption of behavior?

Nowadays, internet is popular, it seems that booking air ticket behavior of using internet is predicted to influence overall tourism air tickets payment method. Tourism industry has grown in the previous several decades. Despite its global impact, questions related to better understanding of tourists and whose habits. Using online travel air ticket booking benefits include booking electronic air tickets can be made from entering any electronic travel agents websites in the short time and electronic travel ticket payers do not need leave home, who can pay visa card to pre booking any electronic travel ticket from online channel conveniently.

How can analyze activity based travel demand ?

Nowadays, human are concerning the traffic congestion and air quality deterioration, the supply oriented focus of transportation planning has expanded to include how to manage travel demand within the available transportation supply. Consequently, there has been an increasing interest in travel demand management strategies, such as congestion pricing that attempts to change aggregate travel demand. The prediction aggregate level, long term travel demand to understanding disaggregate level (i.e. individual levels) behavioral responses to short term demand policies, such as ride sharing incentives, congestion pricing and employer based demand management schemes, alternate work schedules, telecommuting limitation of travel agent traditionally work nature shall influence oriented trip based travel modelling passenger travel demand indirectly.

Finally, online travel purchase will be popular to influence the number of travel behavioral consumption nowadays. Any travel package products can be sold from websites to attract travelers to choose to pre-book air ticket for any trips conveniently. In the past ten years, the internet has become the predominant carrier of all types of information and transactions. Regarding travel decisions, internet has also become an important sales channels for the travel industry, because it is associated with comparably lower distribution and sales costs, but also because it adapts to high supply and demand dynamics in this industry. Consequently, the travel and tourism industry tries to increase the internet sale specific share of sales volumes. So, internet sale channel has changed travel consumption behavioral pattern and characteristics and travel experience. For example, Switzerland has one of the highest population-to-computer ratio in Europe. It is also one of the most highly internet penetrated countries in terms of use of the WWW on a day-to-day basis, with more than 75 percent of the population older than 14 years using the WWW daily (ICT, 2005).

The reason of booking online tourism may include: convenience, fast transaction, finding traveling package choice easily, more airline seats available. So, online booking tourism will influence the traditional tourism agents visiting of sales and air tickets and travelling package numbers to be decreased. Finally, the online booking tourism market shares will be expanded to more than traditional tourism agents visits sale market in the future one day. So, the travel agents who still use the traditional tourism visiting sale channel which ought raise whose features to compare to differ to online tourism sale channel if these traditional tourism agents want to keep competitive ability in tourism industry for long term.

What is actively based patterns of urban population of travel behavioral prediction method?

Actively based patterns of urban population. It is a method of motivational framework means in which societal constraints and inherent individual motivations interact to shape activity participation patterns. It can be used to predict one city or urban the numbers of travel demand in the year. It has two elements: First, capability constraints refer to constraints are imposed by biological needs, such as eating and sleeping and/or resources, such as income, availability of cars etc. to undertake the urban or city's family activities in the year. Second, coupling constraints define where, when and the duration of planning activities that are to be pursued with other individuals. So, this method needs to gather information (data) to get the relationship between activities, travel and spending work time and space time to evaluate whether there are how many families who have real needs to spend time to go to travel in the year.

What is trip based versus activity based approaches?

What is trip based versus activity based approaches? The fundamental difference between the trip-based and activity based approaches is that the former approach directly focuses on trips without explicit recognition of the motivation or reason for the trips and travel. The activity based approach , on the other hand, views travel as a demand derived from the need to pursue travel activities. So, it is better understand the individual or family behavior basis for individual or family travelling decision regarding participation in travelling activities in certain places or cities or countries at given times and hence the resulting travel needs. This behavioral basis includes all the factors that influence the why, how, when and where of performed activities and resulting individuals and household, the cultural/ social norms of the community and the travel surrounding environment.

Another difference between the two approaches is in the way travel is represented. The trip based approach represents travel as a collection of trips. Each trip is considered as independent of other trips, without considering the inter-relationship in the choice attributes , such as time, destination and mode of different trips. As tours are chains of trips beginning and ending at a same location , say home or work. The tour based representation helps maintain the consistency across and capture the interdependency and consistency of the modeled choice attributed among the trips of the same tour.

In addition to the tour based representation of travel, the activity based approach focuses on sequences or patterns of activity participation and travel behavior, using the whole day or longer periods of time is the unit of analysis. Such as approach can address travel demand management issues through an examination of how people modify their activity participation, for example, will individuals substitute more out-of-home activities for in home activities in the evening of who arrived early form work due-to a work schedule change?

The major difference between trip based and the activity based approaches is in the way, the time dimension of activities and travel is considered. In the trip based approach, time is reduced to being simply a cost making a trip and a day's viewed as a combination, defined peak and off peak time periods. On the other hand, activity based approach views individuals' activity travel patterns are a result of their time use decisions with a continuous time domain. As individuals have 24 hours in a day or multiples of 24 hours for longer periods of time and decide how to use that travel among or allocate that time to activities and travel and with who, subject to their socio-demographic, transportation system and other and scheduling of trips. So, determining the impact of travel demand management policies on time use behavior is an important step to assessing the impact of such policies on individual travel behavior. The final major difference between this two approaches relates to the level of aggregation. In the trip based approach, most aspect of travel, e.g. number of trips etc. are analyzed at an aggregate level.

Consequently, trip based methods accommodate the effect of socio-demographic attributes of households and individuals in a very limited fashion, which limits the activity of the method to evaluate travel impacts of long term socio-demographic characteristics of the individuals who actually make the activity travel choices and the travel service characteristics of the surrounding environment. So, the activity based models are better equipped to forecast the longer term changes in travel demand in response composition and the travel environment of urban areas. Also, using activity based models, the impact of policies can be assessed by predicting individual level behavioral responses instead of employing trip based statistical averages that are aggregated over defined demographic segments.

Can apply (AI) big data gathering method predict senior age will be main travelling target?

In the past, Germany government had established tourism survey analysis to analyze survey data in order to arrive at reliable conclusions on future trends in travel behavior. To aim to find how demographic change will influence the tourism market and how the industry can adapt to those changes. The travel analysis provided data on tourism consumer behavior, including attitudes, motives and intentions. Since, 1970 year, it is based on a random sample, representative for the population in private households aged 14 years or older. Then, a continuous high scientific standard combined with a national and international users makes the travel analysis a useful tool and reliable source for tourism industry and policy decisions. It aimed to gather statistical data. e.g. on the age structure and on demographic trends, quantitative and qualitative analysis with time series data from the travel analysis. It shows e.g. not only the future volume , quite different from today's seniors, or how who will travel of family holidays will change, e.g. single parents of low, but grandparents of growing significance for tourism.

Demographic change is said to be one of the important drivers for new trends in consumer traveling change behavior in most European countries

(e.g. Lind 2001). Because the growing number of senior citizens in the European Union and other industrialized countries, such as the USA and Japan, looks to become one of the major marketing challenges for the tourism industry. United Nations statistics predict that the share of people being 60 age or older will grow dramatically in the coming future, and is expected to rise from 10 percent of the world population in 2000 year to more than 20 percent in 2050 year (United Nations Population Division, 2001). From its statistic, some data showed that travel propensity increased throughout life until the age of about 50 years of age and was then kept stable until very late in life 75 age. The most important results is that the travel propensity when getting older is not going down between 65 and 75 age of course, the overall development of this variable is influenced by a lot of other factors which are responsible for quite a variation over time. It is now possible to suggest that the general pattern of travel propensity is one of the key indicators for holiday life cycle travel behavior, includes three stages. The growth stage tends to increase from early adult hood until 45 age old or when reaching some 80%. The next stage is stabilization from the ages of around 50 age, until 75 age old, starting with a lower increase. Finally, the decrease stage is a slight decrease occurs once people reach the more advanced age of 75 age to 85 age old (Lohmann & Danielsson 2001).

So, it seems Germany government tourism prediction to future travelers' behavior indicated these findings, such as on how future senior generations will travel, who had used survey data to examine the patterns of travel behavior of a generation getting older and applied the findings to draw conclusions on the future. Also, it predicted that on the future of family trips, family segmentation will be the travel behavior patterns in the future. These findings together with the statistical data on demographic change allowed for a better understanding of the coming tends in family holidays. It's aim developed in consumer behavior related to demographic change and predicted what will happen future of tourism one had to consider other influences and drivers as well, for example, trends on the supply side. e.g. low cost airlines or in travelling consumption behavior in general whether how the past may provide a key to predict travel patterns of senior citizens to the future.

Given the projected growth of the senior citizens market, designing specific marketing strategies to meet the prospective needs of elderly tourists will become increasingly important. It has been an implicit assumption that it will be a close relationship between the travel behavior of today's senior citizens and the those of future ones. The growing number of senior citizens in the world. e.g. China, Hong Kong, Japan, USA etc. countries. Global senior citizen tourism market will be based solely on demographic predictions about the future of the population's age structure. However, many of these seniors won't only live longer but will be fitter and more active until later in life. Many of the will also have plenty in life. Many of them will also have plenty of time and money to spend on travel. So, will these new seniors behave like today's senior citizens? Will they adopt the same travel behavior as the previous generation or become a new market of oldies for the leisure and tourism industry? However, to determine the actual number of senior citizens who will be travelling and to sought to evaluate and specify certain difficult to predict the actual numbers of senior citizen to any country. However, they can be based on the implicit assumption that there is a close relationship between the travel behavior of past, present and future seniors. But is this a valid assumption? As the revise- analysis travel analysis survey, which was conducted in Germany every year, offered some interesting data possibilities. It was designed to monitor the holiday travel behavior, opinions and attitudes of Germans and has been carried out since 1970 year, questions in the questionnaire. Data are based on face to face interviews, with a representative sample of more than 7,500 respondents, the interviews being carried out in January each year. All results refer to the average for the defined generated, which ranges generally over ten years. The group of people then at the age of 60 to 69 age is described. This corresponds to the same generation ten years ago, when they had an age of 50 to 59 age. When this methodological approach is not necessarily very sophisticated, it does have the important advantages of being cost effective.

IS (AI) big data gathering method a better psychological method to compare human marketing research method predict travel behavioral consumption?

On the psychological view point, I think individual traveler's character will have those kind of personal characteristics. First, simplicity searchers value above everything ease not transparency in their travel planning and holiday making, and are willing to avoid having to go through extensive research. Second, cultural purists use their travel as an opportunity to immerse themselves in an unfamiliar looking to break themselves entirely from their home lives and engage. Sincerely with a different way of living. Third, social capital seekers understand that to be well travelled is a personal quality, and their choices are shaped by their desire to take maximum of social reward from their travel. They will exploit the potential of digital media to enrich and inform their experiences, and structure their adventures always keeping in mind they are being watched by online audiences. Finally, reward hunters seek a return on the investment who make in their busy , high-achieving lives. Linked in part to the growing trend of wellness, including both physical and mental self-improvement who seek truly extraordinary and often indulgent or luxurious' must have experiences.

Why needs to know the personal character of individual traveler's characteristics? Because if travel agents could feel which kinds of individual traveler's character, then who can predict which kind of travel package to design to them more easily. For example, how to determine future travel behavior from past travel experience and perceptions of risk and safety? We need to concern that the influences of past international travel experience, types of risk associated with international travel and the overall degree of safety feeling during international travel on individual's travelling experiences likelihood of travelling to various geographic regions on their next international vacation trip or avoidance of those regions, due to perceived risk. Because individual traveler's experience of safety risk degree to the countries, it will influence who chooses to go to the countries/ country to travel again.

Why travelers avoid certain destinations are as relevant decision making as why who choose to go to the country(countries) to travel. Perceptions of risk and safety and travel experiences are likely to influence travel decisions; efforts to predict future travel behavior can benefit to individual tourist's decision making.

As Weber & Bottom (1989) defined risky decision is as "choices among alternatives that can be described by probability distributions over possible outcomes" (p.114). Some psychologists judge subjective perceptions of physical reality, i.e. image of a particular tourist destination, whereas value judgement refers to the way individual rank destinations according to whose attributes. i.e. attractiveness, safety, risk etc. factors to form on overall image. So, if the individual traveler had unhappy and worried and unsafe experiences to go to where the place(country) to travel during whose vacation time before. Then, this negative travel experience will influence who is afraid to go to the place (country) to travel again. Risk of place, country, destination or region means the danger is relatively high to the place, i.e. increasing in airplane accidents, crime or terrorist activity targeting citizens of potential traveler's nationality or the probability of occurrence is great , i.e. recent occurrences involving travel regions/ destinations under consideration or effective actions to control consequences exist. i.e. selecting safe regions and destinations, taking extra precautions when traveling to risky destinations. These risk factors will influence the individual traveler who chooses to cancel travel plan to go to the country again.

Another interesting research, how to predict behavioral intention of choosing a travel destination, which has focus of tourism research for years, but the complex decision making process leading to the choice of a travel destination has not been well researched. The planned behavior model using its core constructs, attitude, subjective norm and perceived behavioral control, with the addition of the past behavioral variable on behavioral intention of choosing a travel destination.

Understanding why people travel and what factors influence their behavioral intention of choosing a travel destination is beneficial to tourism planning and marketing. Understanding travel motivation is the push and pull model. The idea of the push and pull model is the decomposition of an individual's choice of a travel destination into two forces. The first force is the push factor that pushes an individual away home and attempts to develop a general desire to go somewhere else, without specifying where that may be. The second force is the pull factor, that pulls on individual toward a destination, due to a region specific travel location or perceived attractiveness of a destination. The respective push and pull factors illustrate that people travel because who are pushed by their internal motives and pulled by external forces of a destination. Nevertheless, how push and pull factors guide people's attitude and how these attributes lead to behavioral intentions of choosing a travel destination have rarely been investigated. The decision making process leading to the choice of a travel destination is a very complex process. The planned behavior model is as a research framework to predict the behavioral intention of choosing a travel destination. The model based on the three constructs of attitude, subjective norm, and perceived behavioral control (Fishbein & Ajzen, 1975).

In conclusion, the factors can influence travelers who decide to choose to travel the country, which include personal safety was perceived to the highest motivation factors among the important factors which include, scenic beauty, cultural interests, friendliness of local people, price of trip, services in hotels and restaurants, quality and variety of food and shopping facilities and services. The factors include both push and pull. Push factors include knowledge, prestige, and enhancement of human relationship etc., whereas, the most significant pull factors include high technologic image, expenditure and accessibility etc. For example, Japanese travelers visiting Hong Kong. Push factors are such as exploration dream fulfillment and pull factors are such as benefits sought, attractions and good climate city. It will be the factor of future travel patterns and motivations of sub-cultural and ethic groups for Japanese choice to go to Hong Kong travelling.

How can apply (AI) digital channel (big data gathering method) predict travelling consumer behaviors?

(AI) big data digital channel can be applied to help travelling businesses to evaluate whether how much the e-ticket price and travelling package price is the most attractive or reasonable to persuade travelling consumers feel it is the most reasonable price to choose to buy the airline's e-tickets or the travel agent's travelling package product from internet channel . It helps travelling consumers to feel which airlines or travelling agents which ought change their e-ticket and/or travelling package price to let travelling consumers to choose to buy the airline e-ticket or the travelling agent's travelling package products from internet channel. It can be applied to predict whether how many travelling consumer numbers can be increased or decreased when the airline e-ticket price is variable or the travelling agent travelling package price is variable . It aims to give opinions to help any online airlines or travelling agents to judge whether which e-ticket or travelling package price is the most reasonable to let travelling consumers to accept to choose to buy which airline's e-tickets or traveling agent's package products more attractive.

Thus, (AI) e-ticket or e-travelling package price measurement technology can be preference to be applied online communication ecommerce and mobile phone internet platform aspect. As traveling businesses can enter their past e-ticket or travelling package prices data and past travelling customer number data into computer or mobile. Then, (AI) price measurement technology can gather these data to analyze these e-ticket or travelling package product prices and past travelling customer number to compare their e-ticket and/or travelling package prices variable changing range level to find their e-ticket and /or travelling package price variable difference to measure to make conclusion about every travelling package or/and e-ticket product's price variable changing will influence how many travelling customer number increase or decrease changing to choose to sell their different kinds of travelling package or e-ticket products more accurate. Then, (AI) price measurement software will help them to analyze all past e-ticket and/or travelling package price variable changing data to compare whether which e-ticket and/or travelling package price range can let travelling customers to feel it is more reasonable and attractive to influence them to choose to buy their e-ticket or travelling package product among different airlines and travel agent choices. Because any e-ticket or travelling package product's price is one important factor to influence travelling consumers to choose to buy the airline's e-tickets or travelling agent's travelling package products.

For example, Amazon publish has applied (AI) price measurement technology to help authors to decide how much every different topic of e-book or paper book price, it can attract the largest number of readers to buy. Any one author only needs to type whose book name to Amazon publish author himself/herself Amazon website. Amazon publish (AI) price measurement learning machine will help them to auto-calculate and judge how much e-book or paper book price is the most attractive and the most reasonable in order to increase reader number to buy their e-books or paper books to read. So, (AI) online price measurement machine will gather past similar book names and past every similar book readers' reading times and the number of readers to give opinions to let every author to judge whether his/her very new e-book or paper book ought charge how much price to the e-book or paper book which can attract many readers to choose to buy. Although, it is not ensure that the e-book or paper book price must let readers to feel it is the most reasonable price to choose to buy in reader's view point. However, it has other factors to influence readers' choice to buy the e-book or paper book, e.g. whether the book content is attractive to public, the author's familiarity, the book's page is enough or not to satisfy readers to read etc. factors. But, instead of all these extra factors to influence readers to choose to buy the book to read. (AI) price measurement learning machine can real give opinions to every author to let them to judge the e-book or paper book different price range whether is too high to influence readers to choose to buy to read or tool low to influence readers feel it is possible poor content book to compare other similar content books. Thus, (AI) price measurement machine can help authors to predict every reader's reading behaviors or reading experience and reading habit from online channel in short time easily. The author only enter the book name to let Amazon publish price measurement machine to check, it will follow past reader's reading habit and reading experience to judge whether the similar all book topic sale record to judge how much price is the reasonable price to attract many readers to buy the book.

Hence, (AI) can be applied to digital channel to help travelling businesses to predict travelling consumer behavior in the future. In the future, mobile/smartphone, laptop, desktop will be most frequent used ecommerce channels to develop online business. So, (AI) can be also applied to these platforms to gather data to make analysis to help travelling businesses to predict travelling consumer purchase behaviors popularly. Due to , ecommerce is popular to global, so digital online and instore channels can be one good channel to let (AI) learning machine to make platform to gather past every online travelling consumer purchase (buying) experience data to help travelling businesses to build airline or travelling agent brand personality and having a responsible, positive impact on society.

To apply (AI) learning machine technology to understand travelling customer online purchase behavior, it will raise business e-commerce successful chance: For example, (AI) learning machine can help travelling businesses to gather data to analyze to determine whether short-term or long-term signals in the online travelling consumer behavior that indicate higher purchase intents to let every online travelling business to know. (AI) learning machine can find that online users with long-term purchasing intent tend to save and click through on more content.

However, as online travelling users approach the time of purchase their activity becomes more topically focused and actions shift from saves to searches from online travelling consumption channel. Then, (AI) learning machine will further find that the brand airline and/or travelling agent purchase signals in online travelling consumption behavior can exist weakness before an online travelling purchase is made and can also be traced across different online travelling purchase categories. Finally, (AI) learning machine synthesize these insights in predictive models of online travelling user purchasing intent to the brand of airline or/and travelling agent travelling package product. Taken together, it's work identifies a set of general principles and signals that can be used to model online travelling user e-ticket and/or travelling package purchasing intent across many online content discovery applications. Thus, (AI) learning machine can help online travelling businesses to gather any online travelling users' click online travelling behaviors data to judge whether there are how many online travelling users will choose to find their online travelling business websites to make final decisions to buy their travelling package or/and e-ticket products from online channels. Then, it will give opinions to help the online travelling businesses to let it to judge whether what are the important website factors will help its online travelling business to attract many online travelling consumers, e.g. designing unattractive travelling website issue, online unattractive scene photos issue, unclear website travelling photo color issue, unclear website travelling advertisement message, contents and words impressions issue, lacking image movement frequent attractive seeing issue etc. different website factors. Thus, online digital channel will be one good choice to apply (AI) learning machine to help travelling businesses to predict travelling consumer behaviors.

Thus, (AI) big data technology can also assist travelling consumers to gather different manufacturers' data to compare what their advantages and disadvantages of their travelling package products are. Then, travelling consumers can make comparison to choose which airline or travelling agent is the suitable to whom to buy e-ticket or pre-booking travelling package in online travelling consumption market.

Thus, I believe that artificial intelligent "big data" gathering method can be suggested to be applied to attempt to predict travelling consumer behavioral changes in global online travelling business environment, the reasons are as below:

On the travelling consumer's beneficial hand, travelling consumers can apply this (AI) big data gathering method to attempt to gather any global airline e-tickets and/or travelling agent's package product data to be analyzed by this artificial intelligent learning system to compare human general marketing research method, e.g. survey, questionnaire, marketing plan etc. different human judgement methods to predict traveler consumption behavioral change model. Then, it analyzed all the different data to compare what are the range of the most reasonable e-ticket and/or travelling package online purchase history and sale in order to make more accurate prediction to future traveler change traveling consumption behavioral model in next month, or next half year or next year short term period traveling consumption change prediction.

Reference

Backman and others "motivation is conceptually viewed as " a state of need, a condition that services as a driving force to display different kind of behavior toward certain types of activities, developing preferences, arriving at some expected satisfactory outcome.", 1995, p.15.

Fishbein & Ajzen, "The model based on the three constructs of attitude, subjective norm, and perceived behavioral control". 1975.

Hsu et al. "A tourist behavior model has been developed, called the expectation, motivation and attitude " (EMA) model ,2010.

ICT,WWW . "Switzerland has one of the highest population-to-computer ratio in Europe." Switzerland, 2005.

Jorea Ministry of Environment, " For South Korea environmental attitude is a major factor in decision making vis-a-vis the consumption of " green" food and services", Korea, 2015.

Korea Ministry Of Environment. Public Organizations spend 2.2 Trillon Korean Won To
Purchase green Products in 2014; Ministry Of Environment: Sejoung, Korea, 2015.

Lind , Lohmann & Danielsson , United Nations Population Division, "Demographic change is said to be one of the important drivers for new trends in consumer traveling change behavior in most European countries". 2001.

Mayne, Lonnie. " Evolve of die in the age of the consumer". Entrepreneur, N.P. , 16 Apr. 2014. web of Oct. 2016.

Lee, D.; Kim, M. ; Lee, J. adoption of green electricity policies: Investigating the role of environmental attitudes via big data-driven search-queries. Energy policy 2016. 90, 187-201.

Lee, Terrence, " Tech in Asia-connecting Asia's startup system " Tech. in Asia- connecting Asia's startup ecosystem, N.p.,4 July 2016.

Weber & Bottom "risky decision is as choices among alternatives that can be described by probability distributions over possible outcomes" , 1989, p.114.

Reference
A. Castano et. al. " Automatic detection of dust devils and clouds at Mars" Machine vision and applications, Oct. 2008, vol. 19, no 5-6, pp. 467-482.

Accenture, " Why artificial intelligence is the future of growth"(2017) <http://www.accenture.com/us-en/insight-a   rtificial-intelligence-future-growth>.

D. Schedidt , Unmanned Air Vehicle Command And Control, Handbook Of Unmanned Air Vehicles, Springer-Verlag, 2014. Facebook (AI) Research Available at https://research.facebook.com/ai, research at google, machine intelligence available at http://research.google.com/pubs/machineintellige nce.html; micro soft research-machine learning and artificial intelligence available at http://research.microsoft.com/en-us/research- areas/machine-learning-ai.aspx.

International Federation Of Robotics, 2016. IFR press release world robotics report. IFR, org . 29 Sept. Accessed Feb. 01, 2017. http://www.ifr.org/news/ifr-press-release/world-robitics   report -2016-8321.

K, Fedra , "GIS and environmental modelling" in environmental modelling with GIS, edited by M.F. Goodchild.B.O. Parks and L.T. Steyaert, Oxford University press, pp. 35-50, 1994.

Keynes, J.M. (1933). Economic possibilities for our grandchildren (1930). Essays in persuasion, pp.358-73.

Mckinsey & Company (2013, May). Disruptive technologies: Advices that will transform life, business and the global economy , USA.

Ministry of economy, trade and industry, Japan, 2015, Japan's robot strategy. Ministry of economy, trade and industry.

Ray Kurzweil , The age of spiritual machines (1999) is cited numerously through this chapter: Kurzweilai.net http://www.kurzweilai.net

Rich, Elaine & Knight, Kevin, Artificial Intelligence Second Edition, 1991, New York; Mc-Graw-Hill.

Reference

Camerer, C.F. Babrocks, Loewenstein, G., & Thaler, R. (1997). Labor supply of New York city candrivers: One day of a time. The Quacterly Jounrnal of economics, 112 (2), 407-441. doi: 10.1162/003355399555244.

How do you view the outlook for consumer confidence in your key markets next year? Source from : http://www.Just-food.com Confidence survey, Nov.2015

Jim. P. & Brendan. M. (2013) . What I learned losing a million dollars, p.160. Colimbia University, Columbia business school press, New York, US.

Kamenica, E. (2012). Behavioral economics and psychology of incentives. Annual review of economics, 4 (1), 427-452. doi: 10.1146/annurev- economics-080511-110909.

Maselli, 2012 Technology driven job polarization in EU , 2000-2010. % change in labor supply skilled/upgrade (ISCED) and labor demand for skills/tasks (ISOD).